C000321279

The Papacy and the People of God

The Papacy
and the
People of God

Edited by

GARY MacEOIN

ORBIS BOOKS

Maryknoll, New York 10545

The Catholic Foreign Mission Society of America (Maryknoll) recruits and trains people for overseas missionary service. Through Orbis Books, Maryknoll aims to foster the international dialogue that is essential to mission. The books published, however, reflect the opinions of their authors and are not meant to represent the official position of the society.

Copyright © 1998 by Gary MacEoin

Published by Orbis Books, Maryknoll, NY 10545-0308.

All rights reserved.

No part of this publication may be reproduced or transmitted in any form or by any means, electronic or mechanical, including photocopying, recording, or any information storage or retrieval system, without prior permission in writing from the publisher.

Queries regarding rights and permissions should be addressed to: Orbis Books, P.O. Box 308, Maryknoll, NY 10545-0308.

Manufactured in the United States of America

The papacy and the people of God / edited by Gary MacEoin.
     p. cm.
   Includes bibliographical references.
   ISBN 1-57075-178-1 (alk. paper)
   1. Papacy. I. MacEoin, Gary, 1909-
  BX955.2.P34   1998
  262'.13—dc21   97-39381
                                              CIP

Contents

Introduction

GARY MacEOIN

A book on the papacy is not an alert that a conclave to elect a new pope is around the corner. The moment when a pope has died, or has given clear warnings of imminent death, is the worst possible time for discussion of what is right or wrong with the contemporary form of the papacy. It is a time when short-term issues dominate. Who is the best of the small group of insiders—one hundred twenty or fewer—who constitute the cardinal electors? Which member of this unique club are his colleagues likely to choose?

The issues this book formulates and analyzes are ones best raised when we have a pope who may well continue to preside over the church for years. They are less about the person and style of the present incumbent than about the system built up over centuries within which he functions.

That the papacy needs updating is one issue on which I think there is a clear consensus in the church. As Giancarlo Zizola discusses at some length in Chapter 4, our present pope, John Paul II, has put the issue on the agenda. The church, he said in the encyclical *Ut unum sint* ("That They May Be One": 1995), should search "for a manner of exercising the primacy that would be open to a new situation."

The phrase has the kind of ambiguity that is all too common in Roman documents. In the context, nevertheless, it is clear that John Paul is talking about modifications in papal style and claims that would make primacy more palatable to other Christians. As an initiative, nevertheless, it is not very promising. All it proposes is that the papacy itself undertake its own reform, and if history is clear about anything, it is clear that the papacy does not reform itself. Reform is imposed on it. As historian Paul Collins argues persuasively in his contribution, what this initiative needs is a General Council, a meeting in which the entire People of God would be heard.

The participants in the present study are scattered widely around the globe, each involved in the life of a different local church, a part of the communion of communities that together make up the one holy, Catholic and apostolic church. Each contributor is a theologian or a journalist (or both) with major expertise in the operation of the contemporary papacy. In the preparation of this book no attempt was made to limit individual judgments. All that was asked of each contributor was to present a positive vision of what the papacy can and should be, not only for church members but for all humans.

Given the differences in geographic location, culture, gender, and professional interest, the consensus not only on the need for major changes in the structures and practices of the papacy, but on the form these changes should take, is striking. What I see here is the impact of the Second Vatican Council. Thanks to it, forces have been released in the People of God that cannot be repressed.

Here is the new paradigm of church and church leadership I see sketched in this book. The church must return to many of the structures and practices that defined it in the first centuries, structures and practices that in some—though not all—respects still prevail in our sister churches of the East. The artificial division of the People of God into clergy and laity—nobles and serfs—must disappear. A reformed ministry, a ministry of service and not of domination, will be exercised by leaders chosen by each community without distinction of sex. Doctrinaire concepts of morality, based on a theory of metaphysically fixed essences that is no longer intellectually tenable, will be replaced by a nondoctrinaire notion of nature, in the words of Francis X. Murphy.

This paradigm of church is radically different from that offered by the contemporary papacy. Instead of a central authority in possession of a totality of truth, to be dispensed as that authority deems appropriate, to and through its local agents, we will have a communion of local churches—a "communion of communities," as Pablo Richard expresses it. Each will live and proclaim the faith in its own situation. They will come together with neighboring communities, in progressively larger groups as the needs warrant, to produce not a chorus but a symphony, and to resolve collegially the problems they have in common. That model we already find in the Acts, where Paul goes to Jerusalem and explains to Peter and James how he has adapted Jewish law on behalf of his Gentile converts.

What is envisaged, however, is by no means a future church as a mechanical recreation of the early church. Taking Teilhard de Chardin seriously, we recognize that we humans are engaged in the process of perfecting the human condition, always mindful that this human condition is by definition—because created—less than perfect. It is necessary, accordingly, to look at what has gone wrong with the church since it departed from its original forms and practices, and try to substitute forms and practices designed to prevent future backsliding.

Are there some elements in, or underlying, the contemporary Roman paradigm of church that can be identified as determinant of its nature and that, consequently, must be eliminated if we are to inaugurate a lasting reform? Having reviewed the analyses made by the contributors to this book, I can assert with some confidence that they can all be reduced ultimately to power and control—and perhaps control is nothing more than the exercise of power.

Now, nothing is more obvious than that power corrupts, in church as in society. Jesuit John L. McKenzie expressed what is the view of many when he said that power is the besetting or specific temptation of church authority. "It is not abnormal or surprising that power should be the most seductive temptation for men who have renounced the prospect of wealth and the pleasure of love." All the controls have been put in place to ensure to the leader a monopoly of power: the clerical state, imposed priestly celibacy, and the exclusion of women from leadership.

Here then are three practices that must be changed: the division of the People of God into nobles and serfs, clerics and laity; the obligation of celibacy as a condition of performing priestly duties; and the reservation to men of roles and offices in the church.

I suggest, however, that we go farther. One of the things we have learned from the evolution of civil society is the importance of limiting the terms of office holders. Obviously, the church, like any society, needs officials to preside and to resolve problems and disputes, and, in particular, to preside at the defining act of Christianity, the Eucharist. But they must be accountable to ensure they do not abuse their position. That requires not only election by those over whom they are to preside, but limited terms of office, as well as provision for recall. It means going back to the practice of the early church, but interpreting that practice creatively to match contemporary expectations and needs.

As regards papal elections, many churchmen have recognized the need for some—albeit more limited—reform. Cardinal Michele Pellegrino of Turin proposed in 1966 that the college of cardinals should consist exclusively of the presidents of conferences of bishops, the mandate of each ending when he completed his term of office. Cardinal Leo Suenens of Belgium advanced a similar idea three years later. As part of a broad program of curial reform, he proposed that bishops elect the pope.

Eugene Bianchi and Rosemary Radford Ruether developed these ideas further in a 1992 book, *A Democratic Catholic Church:* "The issue of a democratic Catholic church," they say, "is . . . a crucial hinge for opening the door to further reforms in the spirit of Vatican II." Contributors to that book argue powerfully, as do Bernard Häring and others in the present study, that the current structure of the church is not a mandate from Jesus Christ, but the result of emulating European monarchies of the past. They urge us to reclaim the "dangerous memories" of democracy too long buried in church history.

Such reinterpretation of our earliest Christian practices would mean that the human responsibility for self-development would no longer be seen as purely receptive, but rather as creative. The distinction is important. As Francis X. Murphy explains, the principal reason for the acute and intensifying conflict between Rome's moral teaching and the convictions of Christians based on their lived experience is that Rome is committed to doctrinaire instruction, whereas Christians are engaged in a process of clarification for themselves. Truth is not simply a system of knowledge that only needs to be emphatically taught, as Cardinal Ratzinger's catechism would have it. It is instead attained within a process of self-discovery, behind which stands God's own process of self-revelation.

One monolithic set of structures and practices, as Alain Woodrow insists, does not make sense for a communion of communities containing nearly a billion members spread throughout the world. They belong to diverse cultures and live in different political and economic systems. No one formula is adequate to enable and encourage them to express their emotional, spiritual and religious needs and longings.

This is what John XXIII meant by aggiornamento. As John Wilkins expresses so poignantly, he has not yet been heard in Rome.

Opinion polls and other studies in many countries over several decades have established that an overwhelming majority of Catholics share John XXIII's dream and prayer. In the United States in particular, the sociological facts are unchallengeable. The faithful want to be consulted in the development of teaching about morality. They want election of bishops by the priests and people of each diocese. They want to choose their own pastor. They want not only women altar servers, but women priests and bishops. They want parish councils with decision-making power and control of parish funds. These are not static or declining figures. On the contrary, the demand for change grows in almost direct proportion to Vatican efforts to stifle discussion of these and similar issues. The percentage of the People of God in the United States who want women priests, for example, rose from 29 to 67 in only eighteen years.

In a masterly analysis of papal social teaching, Ana María Ezcurra reminds us that, after more than a century of development, this corpus still suffers from a fatal flaw. Historical and political considerations prevent it from judging with equal objectivity the defects of capitalism and socialism. With the collapse of the Soviet system, it is tempted to accept the claims of the so-called free market neoliberal capitalism to be the only viable economic system. This would be a betrayal of the church's preferential option for the poor, the abandonment to blind economic forces of the vast and growing millions whose very lives are at issue.

There is a radical difference between the Vatican's doctrinaire instructional approach and the communicative approach used by the People of God. We are here facing the fundamental issue of human rights in the church, the denial of which is the main cause of the rising anger and alienation. For the communicative approach, there are no taboo themes. All issues are subject to the process of self-discovery, behind which is the parallel issue of God's self-revelation. It is significant that, for the Vatican, the taboo or nonnegotiable subjects are effectively related to sexuality and to women, in other words, to control and power. They are contraception, homosexuality, divorce and remarriage, ordination of women, married priests, artificial insemination, and abortion. It is hardly surprising that the most fundamental anger today comes from women, an anger that Joan Chittister expresses for us with dignity and passion. Herein lies a major reason why we can hope for change. Until now the institution could count on the unquestioning support of women. The new awareness that identifies patriarchy as the key enemy is changing all that. And not a moment too soon.

The Papacy
and the
People of God

1

Women in the Church

A New Pentecost in Process

JOAN CHITTISTER

"We used to think that revolutions are the cause of change. Actually, it is the other way around," Eric Hoffer wrote in *The Temper of Our Times*. "Change prepares the ground for revolution."[1] The statement intrigues but it also challenges. If it is true, then little or nothing that characterizes this world at the end of the twentieth century can possibly shape it in the next. Change is everywhere and revolution is sure to follow. Even the Roman Catholic Church, one of whose major teachings is its own inerrant indestructibility, finds itself in the crosscurrents of social revolution so great that only change can possibly, it seems, save it from destruction. The questions that follow from such a perspective, of course, are relatively clear and simple ones: What, if anything, can guide the church through this period of massive change and pending revolution? What will remain of the male-defined church as we know it as new ideas develop? What kind of papacy is needed to deal with the woman's issue in a maelstrom of emerging ideas about women? What does that imply for women? More, what does it imply for the church itself which, finding itself on the eve of a new millennium, finds itself as well, in the midst of a revolution it would rather not face?

Despite deep differences in the cultural characteristics that enable various societies to accept and adjust to change, rapid and cataclysmic transformation faces the entire world. In villages where the abacus is still being used as the standard system of commerce, the government that shapes the future of that country is fully computerized. In areas where women are in chadors, women's liberation groups lobby publicly to bring pressure to bear on behalf of the legal rights of married women. In regions where machetes are yet the major agricultural tool, black market arms bazaars are putting the world's most sophisticated weaponry in the hands of teenagers. How can that possibly be and what does it have to do with women, let alone the papacy?

In a century that has seen the coming of compulsory education, globalism, space travel, and cloning, change is the ground on which we live, the soil in which we grow, the air we breathe, and the energy that drives our lives. Revolution rides high on the currents of change and revolution is everywhere. Things once considered immutable are as much in flux now as social fads, ocean tides, and fleeting time. The tectonic plates of the social world groan with the strain of it. China, for instance, that last mysterious behemoth of the ancient world, is revolting from the isolation of past centuries because of the changes around it. Poor peoples—dislocated, destitute, and disregarded—across the world are rising up out of ghettoes, barrios, and rain forests in search of political participation and human dignity, because commercial, economic, and technological changes have made their old world impossible to maintain and the new world inaccessible to them. Death has become an acceptable option for many, no worse than the life they are living now, they say, so whatever the cost to themselves, they intend a different world for their children. With the arrival of space travel and the Hubble telescope, the very perception of humanity about itself has been transformed from earth-bound to cosmic.

These are not cosmetic changes. These are not simply minor shifts in the social climate of a world built around a steady-state system. These are not mere cultural adjustments, the kind that come to nations dealing with an influx of immigrants or the internal reorganization of peoples within a given social stratum. The world in which we live now is not simply moving from dynasty to dynasty, from one empire to another empire, from the use of Latin in a church to the prevalence of the vernacular in liturgical practice. No, what is going on around the globe at this millennial moment in time represents a fundamental shift in the human condition. The very perception of life—its character, quality and meaning—changes from biological development to biological development. The size and complexity of the universe both dwarfs and exalts us, and magnetizes us and makes us cautious. We are less sure than ever of what we really know, or believe, about the ways of the world. The manner in which society interacts, the notion of differences and the traditional concepts of human role responsibilities within the group, open whole new questions and possibilities for personal development. The self-consciousness of the human race itself, once unabashedly anthropocentric, rests now on the well-being of a fish, called the snail darter, and the rest of nature as well. This is a step-over moment in the history of the human race, as major surely as the discovery of the New World with its excursion into new modes of governance. It is obviously as paramount as the development of the printing press with its flood of information, and certainly as important as the emergence of the scientific method and the human control of nature that came with it. It is, in fact, a decisive moment in the development of the human race, one that is changing the way we think, the way we see ourselves, the way we relate to others, and the way we deal with institutions. Oscar Wilde in "The Soul of Man under Socialism" put it this way:

> The systems that fail are those that rely on the permanency of human nature, and not on its growth and development. The error of Louis XIV was that he thought human nature would always be the same. The result of his error was the French Revolution. It was an admirable result.[2]

Changes change things, regardless of social resistance. A whole generation of people do not like computers, for instance, but computers have already changed the way we work, the way we think, and the way we relate to one another. What we like or do not like, in other words, cannot arrest the effects of what we know. Change is not coming; change is here.

No institution need consider itself spared in the process—not the state, not the economic system, and certainly not the church whose theology is daily challenged by changing concepts of creation, of life, and of human nature itself. Nevertheless, the struggle of traditional institutions to maintain the past in the face of a frightening future has seldom been more clear in all of history if for no other reason than because it has seldom been so global. Change is not now simply a national incident, it is an international upheaval the proportions of which are only recently beginning to come into focus. Eruptions in the state, schisms in the churches, and demonstrations in the streets of the world, all attest to the rise and swell of a new consciousness which old systems are neither prepared, nor willing, to accommodate. Corporations duck and feint, and hide and run from the workers of the world to produce the greatest number of goods for the least amount of investment. Fueled by profit rather than justice, their loyalties know no national boundaries. Only now are the poor of the world beginning to realize that their problems do not lie with the poor workers of other countries. Their problems lie with the wealthy corporations of their own countries who move plants and products at will in order to avoid worker compensation laws everywhere. Governments, too, restrain the citizens of the world by want, force, collusion, or lies in order to maintain power that is often bought and always sold to the highest bidder. Religion itself clings to forms that sacralize the system, controlled by priestly castes, rather than to the values within it that could make change a holy and empowering experience for everyone, not simply women. Through it all, men—and men only, in large part—make the decisions, determine the directions, and decide the operations that decide the fate of the rest of the world—plant, animal, mineral, and woman.

Christianity, perhaps, finds itself in a particularly grave situation in the face of changing expectations, understandings, and insights. To preach a God of love who, on the one hand, created women and men out of an identical substance, and a God of power, on the other, whose machoism has supposedly put one gender under the control of the other; to define God as all Spirit, on the one hand, and as exclusively male, on the other; to proclaim a God who makes both men and women in the divine image, but then defines one part of that humanity as less human than the other; to profess a God who calls us all to the knowledge of salvation but gives men alone the right to designate exactly what that means: this implies, requires, and posits a God who is very inconsistent indeed. It is a theological problem of mammoth proportions. And in a world where women, too, get Ph.D.s in theology and philosophy, in science and in history, past answers do not persuade. The woman question is not going to go away no matter how clearly the church says it must. Male hegemony of human thought has had its day. There is another voice to be heard now, rich in experience, full of questions, and very other in its values, goals and perceptions than those touted by a male church throughout two millennia.

Women are intent on bringing their own piece of the wisdom not only to the development of the human race but to the reinterpretation of a faith that once taught racism, anti-Semitism, and slavery with as much confidence as it does sexism in our day. The question, of course, is: How can a church that applies one set of principles to the public arena fail to apply the same set of principles to itself? How can the church call the rest of the world to justice, human rights, political participation and equality for all, while at the same time closing its synods to women, denying its seminaries to women, and reserving its sacristies for men alone—muzzling, in other words, one-half of its own population in the name of God? How can "tradition" possibly be an answer in a church where tradition in every other category is simply the interpretation of the time. This pope, for instance, had no trouble in asserting the equality of women in *Mulieris dignitatem*, despite the church's unbroken theological tradition that had labeled them naturally inferior for centuries.

Fundamentalists, of course, want to call feminist theology, feminist philosophy, and feminist participation in the process of church, heresy. A multitude of historical parallels arise to lend editorial comment and bring discrimination to the discussion. There have been, as a matter of fact, a number of things the church once called "heresy" and punished heretics for believing that have become the theological coin of the realm. Scripture study, for instance, was once considered heresy. It was called "private interpretation" and in defiance of the accepted exegesis of the church.[3] Support for the pluralistic state was called heresy.[4] To believe in the separation of church and state in the face of a theocratic tradition was called modernism and a sin against faith. Acceptance of what Vatican II later termed "whatever else is true" in non-Christian religions was, without reserve, considered heresy. Even participation in the worship services of other Christian churches was considered sinful.[5] Let the thoughtful beware. Such historical perspective taxes a person's patience with decrees designed to deter discussion of one of the most important issues of the time. How Christian is it to agree to say nothing in the face of the primacy of conscience when the greatest moral issues of the moment challenge both the theology and the practice of the church? And if the question

of women can be routinely struck from the agenda of the church by
papal fiat, then why not nuclearism, why not genocide, why not abortion—all of which, among others, deal in one way or another with
questions of creation, life, and power? In fact, why not strike anything
that a pope considers dangerous to the historical grist of the church?

The fact is that two-thirds of the poor of the world are women, two-
thirds of the illiterate of the world are women, and two-thirds of the
hungry of the world are women. There has to be a reason for that.
Oppression of half the human race cannot be explained as an accident.
Oppression is a plan. Oppression is a philosophical position. Oppression is a theological posture, a theological schema, a theological concept made holy because some have said it is so.

The church that purports to witness to the living presence of Christ
in time finds itself with a papacy functioning in the present but, where
women are concerned, embedded in the philosophy, theology, and anthropology of the past. The fact is that the status of women has changed,
if not completely in the structures of the society around them, at the
very least in the minds of women themselves. The church shall not be
spared the revolution that comes from that kind of axiomatic change
in self-perception.

"Woman," it seems is an admissible subject for reflection, discussion, and development everywhere but in the church as we know it in
the twentieth century. And yet, within its very self, the church as we
know it harbors the seed of equality that makes the revolution impera-
tive. At the same time, the church, it seems, is the last institution to
honor it.

The papacy that fails to deal with so fundamental a change in the
perceptions of humankind will be the papacy that presides over the
philosophical demise of the church. Whether or not the church can
possibly last without women is an important but debatable question.
After all, male clubs and sanctuaries have time-honored histories and
may surely survive as some kind of male bonding experience or elite
fraternity. Whether or not the church can possibly live—whole and entire, authentic and true—without women, is not debatable at all. The very
suggestion of such a thing flies in the face of the Jesus-story itself.

The scientific revolution, once the very bastion of the male control
of nature, has in our own lifetime put the lie to male autonomy, to any
autonomy at all as a matter of fact, and to the notion that the world was
made for the disposal of man—identified always as "male" unless spe-

cifically noted otherwise by canons, customs, and papal decrees.[6] With the simple scientific awareness that life is not a ladder but a weave of differences went male pre-eminence, and human primacy as well. Suddenly, the story of creation, and newly rediscovered theological theses with it, drew another look.

Theological Theses. The Genesis 1 story of creation, with its emphasis on man as the crown of creation and creation as a kind of cornucopia filled with the rest of nature for the sake of human satisfaction, became the paradigm of Judeo-Christian thought.[7] Its theme was human transcendence; its thesis was domination. Forgotten, unfortunately, was the correspondingly determinative message that God saw all creation as equally "good," and that the Sabbath—reflection, contemplation, and harmony—not man, was the crown of creation. Gone, as well, were the sobering insights of Genesis 2, that God brings the animals to the human to name, not to give him the right to destroy them, but to require him to understand the depth of the relationship between humanity and those for whom humanity has a personal responsibility, and to whom humanity itself looks for support. The theme of Genesis 2 was companionship; its thesis was human dependency on the rest of creation.

Humanity, and the church as well, built its institutions on Genesis 1. Hierarchy was a given. All things were in the service of men. Males were made in the image of God. Women were made in the image of man. Women were "natural" by virtue of a physiology designed for birthing rather than thinking.[8] Men, on the other hand, whose bodies were not suited for anything inherently creative, must then obviously be suited for the things of the soul; the things of the mind, of course; and the spiritual things of life, obviously. Man/the male was, therefore, closest to God, the theologians argued, because it is the mind that reflects the essential attribute of God—the spirit. In the hierarchy of creation, in other words, instead of gaining because they have both creative body and rational soul, women are defined by their bodies and robbed of the quality of their souls. So spoke Augustine, Origen, and Thomas Aquinas. "Not in the body but in the mind," Augustine wrote, "was man made in the image of God."[9] Woman ("derived," they argued, rather than formed from the same material—"bone of my bone, flesh of my flesh") was made, not in the image of God but in the image of man. So spoke them all. So speak them still.

The thought process is plain: God is utterly other—the ultimate. And so matter, nature, is without value. Nature loses. And woman loses, too.

Francis Bacon's explanation of his scientific method articulated the theology clearly. "Man fell," Bacon explained, "and lost dominion, and can regain dominion through scientific study."[10] Dominion, a male prerogative, became the Holy Grail of a science that had flowered in the service of theology. Then Bacon concluded, "Nature is to be bound into service like a slave."[11] The stage is set. Everything is now in place. What theology asserted, science confirmed. Darwin's Survival of the Fittest fell on ready ears. The Industrial Revolution, colonialism, and "development" became its necessary and dangerous corollaries. Sexism was its given. The world, after all, had been made for humanity, for us, true, but—note well—for the fittest of it. And men, the theologians said, the scientists confirmed, and the philosophers argued, were the fittest of all. Woman is symbol-using, yes, but inferior, intermediate, instrumental. A glorified potted plant. And they said so, these fine philosophers, these holy theologians—all of them. Over and over again.

Philosophical Theses. Jean Jacques Rousseau said a woman could be educated—but not for herself, and not even for the good of society, but only for the advancement of her husband.[12]

John Stuart Mill said a woman could be educated, yes, but only in order to preserve society by being fit to maintain the social standards set by men. An ill-educated wife, he argued, would lead to the deterioration of society.[13]

In 1969, Claude Levi-Strauss said a woman could be educated in order to maintain the domestic system on which men depend to control the public one.[14]

And Pope John Paul II, philosopher, said again in the 1990s that women had "a special nature" for "a special purpose." To maintain the home, apparently, but not the theology of the church.[15]

The patriarchal world view that follows from those premises is a clear one: it is hierarchical in structure, dominative in essence, dualistic in evaluations, and male in its norms. It rests on the premise that some of us were made to be—are meant to be—better than the rest of us, that some of us are in charge of the human race and we know who we are. It is, in other words, a recipe for conflict, struggle, sexism, racism, suppression, oppression, and revolution. And we are in it. And it is everywhere. And it has come to white heat in our day, in our time, in this century.

Structural Implications. The results of a thought process based on domination is a clear one. The dualism that defines women as "natural" rather than spiritual, and nature as inferior in the face of the all-spiritual God, makes a clear distinction between the social roles of women and men. Women are born for child-bearing, "mothering" is their lifetime task and serving the needs of men is—like the rest of nature—their primary function. Men, men said, exist to dominate the realm of ideas, to determine the operations of life, and to enjoy the fruits of nature. For them, fathering is an event. Echoes of these ideas ring in every debate of its kind to this day. Institutions are shaped by them. The church encourages them. The Jesus whose ministry was supported by women, spread by women, announced by women, and shared by women finds little to recognize in the designs of nature here.

Women, not made of sacred substance, the arguments imply, have no part of sacred things in a cosmogony such as this. Woman's domain is domestic. Woman's legal rights are limited. Women need men, literally, to be their "heads." The capstone to the argument is a simple one: God did it this way and so, clearly, God wants it this way. Try as they might, there is nothing men can do about the matter to situate women in the same human position as men. As if they were not, in the first place, themselves responsible for an interpretation of scripture that makes it so.

Throughout the world to this day, men control the public sphere and all the laws that the public sphere develops to control both nature and women. Since men, the males of the species, are normative, they know what is good for everyone and everything else. The conundrum, of course, is that science has betrayed the triumvirate of philosophy, theology, and anthropology. We know that men are mightily natural and women are clearly rational. We know now that we can't have it both ways. Either women are different and must, therefore, be heard from out of their own experience, as subjects, not objects; as moral agents, not as moral minors—or women are the same, and hearing from them is to be taken for granted. As it is, the gifts of women are, for the most part, being lost to society as a whole, and to the church, in particular, where the spirituality of women has long been the backbone of the faith.

But with the pillars of hierarchical thinking weakened on every side, there is no justification for the suppression of peoples and no way to sustain that suppression other than through brute force. Change has begun the revolution. The confinement of women as a class to the domestic dimensions of society rings false.

A New Papacy for Women. The problem for women in a church in the midst of change is that they live with a papacy that theoretically belongs to the last century, canonically governs in the present, and provides for the future out of an anthropology now defunct. Both science and philosophy have now denied the kind of hierarchical, dualistic definitions of life that have sustained domination throughout the first millennium. What we need now is theological leadership that will do the same. We need a papacy that can see the oppression of women by the church itself and is willing to model their inclusion at the highest levels of Vatican planning. The implications of that for the church, however, are major. Words alone will not do. The next papacy will be required to demonstrate a clear acceptance of the equality of women or the credibility of the church in a world awakening to equality, all the way from the Little League baseball teams of the Western world to the parliaments of world governments, will be severely, if not mortally, compromised. The notion that God does not want for the church what God apparently wants everywhere else in humankind, strikes a specious chord on the human ear. The implications are clear.

The Theological Insights of Women Must Be Recognized. For two thousand years the thinking of the church has been almost exclusively male. Little or nothing of women's experience, interpretation, and insights has been incorporated into official church documents. The truth of the matter is that the Catholic church operates as if women are not in it. The effect on women has been negative, of course, but the effect on the church has been worse. Under no condition can it claim to have seen Jesus, the Christ, with two eyes.

If women are really reasonable creatures, however, then they are theology-thinking human beings. That theologizing must be fostered, recognized, and heard. The next papacy must name women to all theological commissions, encourage their presence on seminary faculties around the world, seek their interpretations and listen intently not only to their emerging questions, but to their answers to theological issues as well. When early theologians—Clement, Origen, Augustine, Anselm, John Climacus, and a multitude of others—engaged in heated exchange over issues basic to the faith, the process met with respect. The church weighed each position thoughtfully and seriously. Now, women must be included in that same theological debate with that same sincerity or the work of the church is only half finished.

To design the doctrines of the church on salvation, sexuality, marriage, family, and sin—all of which affect the lives of women equally but differently than they do the lives of men—without formative input from women themselves, conveys positions that are incomplete as well as arrogant. The continuing questions of women over time have pointed out the fault lines of the faith. The theological answers of women to the theological questions of the age may demonstrate both its partisanship and its plausibility as well. Until then, the answers of male theologians to women's questions will remain forever suspect. When the Canaanite woman challenged the justice and theology of Jesus toward outsiders, it was a process of conversion that took place—both his and hers—not authoritarianism or oppression.

The question "What do the scriptures say to women?" needs to become a part of every course, a concern in every document, a clue to deeper meanings and a guide to more meaningful insights for the church at large, if scripture is ever to reveal itself to the whole Christian community. Scripture study that excludes women at the highest levels of discourse is study that hears, sees, and feels only one-half of the message in the material. The leadership of Miriam, the autonomy of Mary, the commissioning of the Samaritan woman, the teaching of Martha, have for far too long been ignored or, at best, only superficially accounted for by standard male exegeses. Tomes have been written, for instance, on the stoning of Stephen or the identity of the unnamed young man in the Garden of Gethsemane, but hardly a word on the saving of Moses by two women—two enemies, two subverters of the system they both rejected, one the slave, the other the princess. A great deal has been inferred about the priests of Baal, and almost nothing about the Jewish midwives, Shiphrah and Puah. It is time to see the women in scripture as much the messengers of God, the leaders of the people, and the saviors of the faith, as the men were.

The Spiritual Insights of Women Must Be Made Available to the Entire Church. The church needs women as spiritual directors. The papacy of the next millennium must take special care to include the spiritual insights of women in the direction of the church. Feminist spirituality is as essential for men as it is for women because it develops an entirely new world view, in contradiction of the values spawned by patriarchy and institutionalized in the church. Feeling, compassion, inclusiveness, community, and globalism, among others, must begin to bring balance to the kind of cold rationality, individualistic asceticisms, elitism, authoritarianism, and autonomy that have characterized spirituality in the past.

Women spiritual directors must certainly become part of every seminary program, every chancery office, every spirituality course taught, and every diocesan retreat given. Priests especially—not a caste above the average thinking, serving Christian—must have the opportunity to work with women spiritual directors if, for no other reason, than to develop their own sensitivities to the point where they can minister to women at large comprehendingly and respectfully. To be in a church where official Vatican directives deny a seminarian the right to have a mature woman as a spiritual guide is a very clear signal that the men of the church have nothing whatsoever to learn about the faith from the women of the church. It is a clear message, and a false one. The question that follows then, for women is, "Why stay?"

The Ecclesiastical Leadership of Women Must Be Institutionalized. The Roman Catholic Church, universal in definition, human in scope, has no right to be either a male or a clerical preserve. The church is not male. It simply looks that way. In order to develop a real Christian community—one that thinks and acts and witnesses together— the synods of the church must include women, the curial congregations of the church must be headed by women, the cardinalates of the church, until 1917 granted to laity as well as to clerics—Giovanni de Medici in the fifteenth century and Giacomo Antonelli in the nineteenth, for instance[16]—must be opened to women, as well. Diocesan offices and parishes must be routinely pastored by dedicated women whose commitment to living the Gospel by participating fully in the church is not hindered by the church itself. The next papacy to be credible in a changing world will need to demonstrate within itself what will soon be common coin around the world—the human community in tandem, learning from one another, supporting one another, respecting one another, and loving one another to fullness of life.

The Ordination Question Must Be Allowed the Impulse of the Spirit. To deny the church as a whole the right to discuss the issue of either women deaconesses, women priests, or a married clergy, speaks of the flimsiness of the theological positions which underlie the canonical definitions at the present time. To risk the loss of the sacraments in a sacramental church by preferring maleness to priesthood is a breach of faith even more serious, perhaps, than simple authoritarian administration. Finally, to confuse the Jesus of history with the Christ of faith—to make Eucharist a mime rather than a sacrament—and so to deny half the human race the right also to "remember Him" when they gather, makes for very profound theological concerns.

Respected theologians everywhere admit the validity of the questions. Protestant Christianity, prophet to the Roman Catholic Church for centuries by virtue of its preservation of scripture study, may well now be required to preserve the Eucharist as well unless something is done to free it from its male confines. Clearly, the church in the next millennium needs a papacy willing to trust the movement of the Spirit on these issues before the Christian community dissolves into a collection of distant individuals and Eucharist itself becomes, at best, only a pallid memory of a faith once vital but now defunct.

"A living thing is distinguished from a dead thing," Herbert Spencer wrote in his 1864 landmark volume, *Principles of Biology,* "by the multiplicity of the changes at any moment taking place in it."[17] We are dangerously past due some important changes, perhaps, if we want to do more than exist as a church. The next papacy will not be responsible for the administration of the church. The next papacy will need, where women are concerned, to breathe some life back into it.

The Question of the Nature of God Must be Revisited and Publicly Reshaped. If women are to find themselves in the church, they must be able to find themselves in the Godhead, as well. God-language that requires the all-spiritual God to be "father," and denies the womb and breasts of God of which Deuteronomy, Isaiah and the psalmist speak, smacks of the heretical itself. The church that is willing to call God a hundred names—rock, key, door, root, hen, and tree—but never, ever "mother," needs a thorough examination of conscience. There must be a reason to need to skew, contradict, and contort the obvious with such vehemence. It is time to determine, to face, and to repent the kind of sexism that fears the feminine, even in God. There must be something in the male psyche of the church that insists on projecting onto the female its fears of itself. God-language itself unmasks the fragmentation in the church's understanding of God. It is time for the church to become whole. It is time for the papacy to lead us out of such a tangled theological morass, back to the Jesus of lepers and outcasts and women, of beseeching women and proclaiming women and ministering women, of women with reckless faith, and of women with fearless presence and interminable fidelity.

We need a Pentecost papacy in the next millennium that can hear the many voices of women—each speaking in her own tongue—and understand them.

The time is short. After all, as Hoffer taught us, "We used to think that revolutions are the cause of change. Actually, it is the other way around. Change prepares the ground for revolution." And change is here—whether the papacy is ready for it or not.

Notes

1. Eric Hoffer, "A Time of Juveniles," in *The Temper of Our Times* (New York: Harper & Row, 1967).

2. Oscar Wilde, "The Soul of Man under Socialism," in *Fortnightly Review* (London, Feb. 1891; reprinted, 1895).

3. Wolfgang Bienert and Francis Schüssler Fiorenza, eds., *Handbook of Catholic Theology* (New York: Crossroad, 1995), pp. 650-652; also Raymond Collins, "Scripture, Interpretation of," in *Encyclopedia of Catholicism* (San Francisco: Harper Collins, 1995), pp. 1173-1175.

4. J. Bryan Hehir, "Church and State," in *Encyclopedia of Catholicism*, pp. 314-317.

5. Stanislaus Woywood and Callistus Smith, *Practical Commentary on the Code of Canon Law* (New York: Joseph F. Wagner, 1952), p. 513.

6. John B. Cobb, Jr., "Ecology, Science and Religion: Toward a Postmodern Worldview," in Mary Heather MacKinnon and Moni McIntyre, eds., *Readings in Ecology and Feminist Theology* (Kansas City: Sheed and Ward, 1995), pp. 236-238.

7. Michael J. Himes and Kenneth R. Himes, "The Sacrament of Creation: Toward an Environmental Theology," in Mary Heather MacKinnon and Moni McIntyre, eds., *Readings in Ecology and Feminist Theology*, pp. 272-274.

8. Joan Chittister, OSB, *Heart of Flesh: A Feminist Spirituality for Women and Men* (Grand Rapids: Eerdmans, 1997), p. 32.

9. Augustine, *Commentary on the Gospel of John*, XXIII 10, as quoted in Grace M. Jansen, "Healing Our Brokenness: The Spirit and Creation," in Mary

Heather MacKinnon and Moni McIntyre, eds., *Readings in Ecology and Feminist Theology*, p. 285.

10. Francis Bacon, *Novum Organum* (Works, Part 2, Vol. 4, p. 247), as cited in Carolyn Merchant, "Feminists Perspectives on Science," in Mary Heather MacKinnon and Moni McIntyre, eds., *Readings in Ecology and Feminist Theology*, pp. 338-341.

11. Francis Bacon, *The Great Instauration*, written 1620 (Works, Vol. 4, p. 20), as quoted in Carolyn Merchant, *The Death of Nature: Women, Ecology and the Scientific Revolution* (San Francisco: Harper Collins, 1983), p. 169.

12. Moira Galens, *Feminism and Philosophy: Perspectives on Difference and Equality* (Bloomington: Indiana University Press, 1991), p.17.

13. Galens, ibid., p. 30.

14. See Claude Levi-Strauss' argument in *The Elementary Structures of Kinship* (Boston: Beacon Press, 1969).

15. Pope John Paul II, *Mulieris dignitatem*, 15 August 1988, in *The Pope Speaks*, 34 (1989), pp. 10-47.

16. *Encyclopaedia Britannica*, 15th ed., "Leo X" (Giovanni de Medici) and "Giacomo Antonelli" (Vol. 7, pp. 274-275, and Vol. 1, pp. 465-466).

17. Herbert Spencer, *Principles of Biology*, Part 1, Chap. 4 (1864).

2

My Hope for the Future
of the Petrine Ministry

BERNARD HÄRING, C.Ss.R.

A sudden hope filled me, as I watched in 1978, while John Paul II was being installed as pope. After the oft-quoted, "you are Peter, and on this Rock I will build my Church," I heard the warning, "get behind me, Satan, you are a scandal." Will this papacy, I asked myself, initiate a truly biblical and ecumenical renewal of the Petrine Ministry?

The past two decades, however, have disillusioned me. An increasingly uncompromising Vatican centralism, together with punitive control mechanisms, have dashed my expectations. We must still hope, nevertheless, that John Paul will go down in history for his courageous encyclical, *Ut unum sint* ("That They May Be One"), a prophetic sign, an invitation to all Christians to join in a search for a universally acceptable Petrine ministry.

I have intentionally said "Petrine Ministry" rather than papacy. Overtones associated with the latter word unfortunately inhibit authentic attempts at dialogue.

Motivated by Vatican Council II's ecumenical advances, many Catholics entertain an ardent desire for a Petrine Ministry in keeping with the gospel, the primitive church, and the signs of the times. The many Christians represented by the World Council of Churches, a body that has removed all major obstacles to Christian unity, share that desire.

Vatican II, supported by John XXIII and Paul VI, called for elimination of more than minor defects. We need a conversion and struc-

16

tural changes in the papal office to return us to the biblical beginnings and the historical experiences of the first Christian centuries.

THE PETRINE PICTURE IN THE BIBLE

The New Testament's astonishingly meaningful picture of the person of Peter and his original activities helps us understand his specific ministry. That Jesus entrusted him with a specific ministry is beyond doubt. Peter shows himself as spontaneous. He possesses initiative and goes directly to Jesus, his master, on occasions that were decisive for the working of the Spirit. Still, his betrayal, resulting from a false, all-too-earthly misunderstanding of the Messiah, is shocking. Jesus qualified it as "a Satanic scandal."

Seeing through Peter's appalling lack of understanding, however, Jesus promises him a fundamental conversion. The Acts of the Apostles (1:15-26), for example, depicts Peter's role in electing a replacement for Judas Iscariot. Having announced that the symbolic number Twelve has to be restored, he leaves the search to the whole community. And when two acceptable candidates are identified, instead of hazarding his authority, he gladly has the issue decided by drawing lots.

Peter and the primitive church were not shocked when Paul "opposed him to his face" on an important question, since Peter was at fault (Ga 2:11). At the so-called Council of Jerusalem in 51 A.D. Peter plays an enabling role, but again without exercising decisive authority. Earlier he had opened a new perspective by baptizing the pagan Cornelius and his whole family (Ac 10:2). Nevertheless this does not give the impression that Paul had taken precedence because of his pioneering activity.

The bishop of Rome performed a special function from the beginning—not, however, as successor of Peter, but because both Peter and Paul had preached the gospel and given witness with their martyrdom in Rome. He clearly exhibited a responsibility for the entire church, as did the patriarchs of Antioch, Alexandria, and Jerusalem.

WORLDLY TRAPPINGS AND RIDICULOUS TITLES OF HONOR

The church is neither a monarchy nor an oligarchy. It is, as Vatican II declares, the pilgrim "people of God," exemplary through its intimate relationships, its history, and its ability to dialogue with confidence in the workings of the divine Spirit "in all and through all," and always in full view of all.

Since Constantine, however, the church has gradually taken on monarchical—even at times absolutistic—structures, worldly trappings, triumphalistic pomp, and ridiculous titles of honor. Equally harmful to its image has been the tendency to sacralize these propensities. The church that so convincingly calls for conversion of the individual must recognize that the church itself needs an in-depth renovation of structures and forms of address and mindsets—in a word, an authentic conversion.

Over the last century the church has created a sound social ethic with the basic principles of solidarity and subsidiarity. Current structure and practices, nevertheless, involve activities that progressively contradict these principles. Everything in its government and teaching comes from the top down, from above to below, with singular tendencies to monopolistic power. It even claims a monopoly of the Truth and an all-embracing method of interior control.

At Vatican II, the church had declared itself explicitly as a synodal or collegial structure. Yet the Roman Synods of Bishops, being limited to an advisory role, have had almost no influence. Their majority decisions are treated as simply non-binding. The 1980 Synod, for example, decided almost unanimously that the Roman Catholic Church could, in its pastoral care of the divorced and remarried, follow the example of the *oikonomia* or practice of the Orthodox churches. The Synod's conclusion, as set out in the encyclical *Familiaris consortio*, was more than surprising. There the Pope decided—without explanation or advice—that the divorced could not under any circumstances receive the sacraments without a declaration of nullity.

Vatican I had placed clear limitations on papal infallibility. Without the explicit inclusion of these limitations, the constitution *Pastor Aeternus*—on papal infallibility—could not have won the necessary votes. Pope John Paul's declaration that women cannot be ordained as priests was at first labeled definitive, then upgraded by the Congregation for the Doctrine of the Faith to infallible. It is evident, however, to the countless dissenting men and women theologians and many bishops, that the means provided by divine providence to ensure the entire church's participation were not employed before the papal declaration. We need no change in the dogma of infallibility, merely its authentic interpretation. Only thus will it be clear that the papal magisterium is fully joined in solidarity with the church's worldwide faith community.

What Vatican I taught on the primacy of papal jurisdiction is still in effect; and it is bound in with the notion of collegiality in all phases of the church's being. This was a singular concern of Vatican II.

The papacy, nevertheless, remains a serious obstacle, one that can be overcome only by a new praxis that observes the principle of subsidiarity. No explanations of papal rule can overcome this obstacle to unity as long as such practices as Rome's naming and deposing of bishops are continued.

In the church's early centuries no one thought that the bishop of Rome should name other bishops. Even today no such idea—let alone practice—exists in any of the principal patriarchates of the East.

Centralized bishop-naming and its accompanying system of central control is a carry-over from an era of political centralism and authoritarianism. In today's democratic culture that recognizes the principle of subsidiarity for the whole secular world (including the papacy), this system constitutes a serious case of historical alienation.

John Paul II applies a simple criterion in naming bishops, and in the rigid control of male theologians (and even more of female theologians): a strict conformity with his interpretations on contraception, the pastoral care of the divorced and remarried, and the irrevocable exclusion of women from priestly ordination.

For selecting bishops, the starting point should be the practice of the first thousand years. One single process or pattern is not needed for the entire church.

Bishops' conferences can now fulfill the function of the ancient patriarchates, setting the rules not only for naming bishops but for such activities as certifying theology professors. Canon law for the entire church can and should be less rigid. Synodal structures must be strengthened and be seen to function everywhere, thus assuming different forms in various cultural situations. Watchfulness and responsibility must replace the centralized control system.

PAPAL ELECTIONS

Peter's successor is more than a mere symbol of unity. His office is a positive service to the unity of all Christians. Because of the colle-

gial nature of the office, we cannot go back to the election of the bishop
of Rome by the Roman clergy along with the Roman people and neighboring bishops. Electing a pope is a universal church activity of the
highest importance.

The process has a rich history with light and dark sides. The circle
of electors was gradually widened, but it was not until Nicholas II
(1059) and Alexander III (1179) that the cardinals became the sole
electors, a process that developed by analogy to and in imitation of the
monarchical heredity principle. The cardinals, then few in number,
were considered the "sons" of the pope, who thus created a dynasty by
naming a small circle of heirs.

The history of the predominance of the cardinals—as well as rela-
tives and so-called celibate "sons"—in selecting the pope includes
periods that were utterly shocking, the atmosphere of the gospel hardly
recognizable.

Given the pope's fundamental role as bishop of Rome, it would be
appropriate that the Eastern churches and the traditional metropolitan
churches in communion with Rome be invited to make specific suggestions for future elections, and also contribute some of the electors.

The presidents of the world-wide Conferences of Bishops should
likewise participate in the church's selection of a new pastor, as should
outstanding men and women. That women be included seems to me an
unavoidable advance on the realization of the Petrine Ministry for the
entire people of God, in view of the updating of the church in keeping
with the signs of the times.

THE PETRINE MINISTRY

Given the universal desire for Christian unity, the Petrine Ministry
is more important today than ever before. For the sake of its gospel-
oriented form, the Petrine Ministry must be fundamentally simpler
than the tradition-burdened papacy. Its qualifications should not go
beyond the talents of a well-endowed individual.

This ministry must be completely freed of historically foreign ac-
cretions, from secular decorations and ridiculous pomp. Titles such as
"Your Holiness" belong to the past. How grotesque it is for the pope to
name "Prelates of Honor" to "His Holiness"! Everything about such
titles is false. Prelate signifies predominance over others; and the pope
calls himself "My Holiness"!

Not only must the pope not name any more "wearers of the Purple," he must also end the whole complicated and often ridiculous system of titles of honor and advancements. The sophisticated system of rewards and punishments in the papal service has endangered the purity of motives. The future pope must renounce his role as a political leader among world rulers, an action that will eliminate the entire system of nunciatures. The witness of the gospel will be stronger when pope and bishops refrain explicitly from political involvements.

Liaison of local churches with the papacy will then be maintained by the bishops' conferences who will send representatives to the Apostolic See. Channels of information will inevitably be more open and free of political interference.

Many people believe that the Catholic church, in view of its ecumenical commitment, should courageously reconsider the two dogmas defined by Vatican Council I, namely, infallibility and papal primacy. In my considered opinion this is not necessary. It would suffice—and be universally useful—if the entire church, and in particular the pope, realistically recognized the principle of subsidiarity. The pope's authority could then be reserved for the most pressing emergencies, retaining its validity without any suspicion of a desire for power or predominance.

Regarding infallibility, I have already compared this dogma to a safety net put together by Vatican Council I in its final hours with its Dogmatic Constitution, *Pastor Aeternus*.

Vatican II insisted emphatically that the Petrine Ministry and the papal magisterium are linked indissolubly to the belief of the entire people of God. This linkage includes the collegial activity and teaching of the whole college of bishops with the pope as its head.

In consequence of the many outspoken personal positions I have taken, I believe I should make myself perfectly clear. A radically renewed Petrine Ministry means much more for the entire church and for the re-establishment of Christian unity than a tradition-bound papacy.

—Translated by Francis X. Murphy

3

Infallibility, Primacy, Magisterium, and Reception

PAUL COLLINS

PERCEPTIONS OF PAPAL POWER[1]

Popular perceptions are not theology, but they do give us access to the way in which belief and doctrine are understood by most people. One widespread belief, both inside and outside Catholicism, is that the papacy and the church are coterminous. Many people think that everything the pope says is absolute law for "good Catholics," and that the pope controls the church totally. The popular perception is that Catholics cannot disagree in any way with the pope, or dissent from his priorities.

This image of the papacy, built up over more than a century, has been reinforced by the high profile of the present pontiff. Pope John Paul II has achieved a centralization of papal power unmatched in history.

Usually the doctrine of infallibility is taken as the summation of papal authority. This is incorrect, for the definition of infallibility is actually hedged in with severe restrictions. The bishops at the First Vatican Council (1869-1870) were careful to define exactly what they meant by infallibility and they stipulated precisely the conditions under which it could be exercised. In fact, it is rather difficult for the pope to act infallibly. At Vatican I there was a sizeable minority of bishops who forced a prolonged and serious debate about infallibility. No such care was taken, however, with papal primacy, an issue on which the minority bishops were less focused. Yet it is primacy that has created most subsequent problems. It has led to the exercise of untrammeled papal power and has become a major stumbling block in ecumenical relationships with both the Orthodox (who consider the definition to be heresy) and the Protestants.

VATICAN I AND *PASTOR AETERNUS*

The conciliar teaching on infallibility and primacy is set out in the dogmatic constitution *Pastor Aeternus* (18 July 1870).[2] The constitution clearly defines infallibility. When the pope speaks *ex cathedra,* as pastor and teacher of the church, on issues of faith or morals, it says he speaks infallibly because he shares in the divine assistance promised to Peter and bestowed by Christ.[3] This is not a personal gift; it can only be exercised within the context of the church when the pope speaks as "shepherd and teacher of all Christians." No pope can speak as a private theologian, nor can he make his personal opinions normative. He must always speak within an ecclesial context and give voice to the belief of the church.[4]

Unfortunately, this unequivocal context was muddied at the last moment by the introduction of a sentence that attempted to exclude the Gallican position held by a couple of French bishops at the Council. Gallicanism maintained that the pope was only infallible if the broad church community gave subsequent assent to his teaching. The sentence excluding Gallicanism is badly formulated, and it says that the pope's definitions are irreformable *ex sese, non autem ex consensu ecclesiae* ("of themselves and not from the [subsequent] consent of the church"). This sentence, in isolation, could be interpreted to imply that the pope was infallible of himself and that he did not have to make sure that he was teaching what the church believed and taught. The phrase also seemingly contradicts the well-established doctrine of reception. The very danger that many bishops at the Council feared— that the pope would become an ecclesiastical oracle—was opened up by this attempt to exclude Gallicanism.

The conciliar teaching on primacy is found in chapter three of *Pastor Aeternus*. Clearly primacy is an ancient doctrine, something that no one at the Council disputed. But what did the concept mean and how was it to be defined? It was a debate that had long constellated around three questions: the extent and limit of papal jurisdiction, the sense in which papal and episcopal power coexisted, and the relationship of a pope to an ecumenical council.

None of these historical questions was dealt with adequately at the First Vatican Council. They were side-stepped, largely because an ideological rather than an historical hermeneutic dominated the thinking of the majority at that Council. Basically, what was defined was that Peter, as head of the apostles, had true and proper jurisdiction bestowed on him by Christ, a jurisdiction that is passed on to the bishops of Rome. *Pastor Aeternus*, drawing on an ancient tradition, says that Peter lives on in his See in an almost sacramental sense: "To this day and forever [Peter] lives and exercises judgement in his successors, the bishops of the Holy Roman See. ... Blessed Peter perseveres in the rock-like strength he was granted and does not abandon the guidance of the church which he once received."[5]

Traditionally the pope is more the "vicar of Peter" than the "vicar of Christ," a term that came into widespread usage only with Innocent III (1198-1216). The conciliar teaching then continues in legal rather than theological language; it says that the Roman church possesses "a pre-eminence of ordinary power" that is "episcopal and immediate."[6]

It is significant that primacy is defined in terms of power and jurisdiction and not in terms of leadership. The definition stresses that the pope has authority over the ecclesial communion rather than that he provides a service of unity to it. The two words "ordinary" and "immediate" are canonical words connoting the fact that the power intrinsic to the office comes to the elected individual with the bestowal of the office. This universal power of jurisdiction is "full and supreme" in matters of faith and morals, as well as in everything that concerns the discipline and government of the whole church and everyone in it.[7]

The phrase *plenitudo potestatis* ("the fullness of power") excludes the Gallican position which argued that the pope had the principal power, but not the fullness of power in the church. Unfortunately, what is suggested by the text of *Pastor Aeternus* is that there are no limits to papal power, and certainly since 1870 this has been the popular perception. The reason why the bishops of Vatican I were far less nuanced in the definition of papal primacy was clearly recognized at the time: the theology of the church shared by the majority of the conciliar fathers was defective. The English historian, Cuthbert Butler, comments that a group of bishops were concerned that the episcopate was entirely neglected in *Pastor Aeternus*. "Here is a summary of Catholic doctrine on the church in which there is no account taken of the hierarchy, episcopate, ministry, and ecumenical councils—simply church and pope."[8] *Stupefacti sumus* ("We are astonished!"), exclaimed one bishop.[9]

After the papal definitions the Council was suddenly prorogued because of threats to the city from the forces of the *Risorgimento*. Rome was occupied by Italian troops in September 1870 and no attempt was made by Pius IX (1846-1878) to recall the Council. He had achieved his aims: infallibility and primacy had enhanced papal power without any corresponding theological or ecclesial context. Like most contemporary bishops, Pius IX saw the definitions in apocalyptic terms: they were bulwarks against the "demonic forces" of liberalism, democracy, and the modern world. Instead, the definitions have now created an ecumenical and constitutional crisis for the church itself.

THE CONSEQUENCES OF *PASTOR AETERNUS*

Between the First Vatican Council and the Second Vatican Council (1962-1965) the equation, that the pope equals the church, went unchallenged. Attempts were made at Vatican II to right this imbalance through the formulation of the doctrine of episcopal collegiality and the enhancement of the role of the laity. Certainly the teaching of Vatican I must be read within the context of Vatican II. Vatican I was the final product of a millennium of western isolation from the eastern churches which always had much stronger episcopal and synodal traditions. At Vatican II there were both Orthodox and Protestant observers present and they exerted an influence on the formulation of the Council's documents. Vatican II also had the advantage of a better articulated and more traditional ecclesiology which had been developed in the previous decades through a renewal of patristic studies and a clearer sense of the historical development of doctrine. At Vatican II the historical hermeneutic predominated over the ideological.

Since Vatican II, nevertheless, this more participative vision of church polity has not been realized in ecclesiastical structures. The papacy of Paul VI (1963-1978) was characterized by ambivalence and a failure to make the hard, practical decisions that would have been necessary in order to take seriously the ecclesiology of Vatican II. At-

tempts were made to establish a synod of bishops, but these were ham-
strung from the start by papal control of agenda and topics. The papacy of John Paul II (1978-   ) has led to a more extreme situation
than that which obtained before Vatican II. Under Paul VI there was a
tinkering with the structure of the Roman Curia, but no attempt was
made to force this body to take seriously the new ecclesiology. The
only way now to reform this cumbersome and unnecessary curial bureaucracy is to abolish it.

THE ORIGINS OF INFALLIBILITY

The origins of the doctrine of infallibility are recent by the ancient
standards of church tradition. At Vatican I it was assumed that the
doctrine went back to the beginning of the church, and it was wrongly
argued that silence on infallibility in the first millennium indicated
that the doctrine was universally accepted. Brian Tierney has recently
shown that the doctrine first emerged in the fourteenth century in the
convoluted dispute among the Spiritual Franciscans over evangelical
poverty.[10]

Popes such as John XXII (1316-1334) rejected the notion of infallibility because, as John correctly perceived, it restricted the power of
popes by binding them to their predecessors' decisions. In the twelfth
century the canonist Gratian distinguished papal jurisdiction from
church indefectibility. He held that the pope had the right to pronounce
on disputed matters of faith, but that he could and did err. For Gratian
the key issue was Christ's promise to Peter that the church would always survive.

Despite criticism, Tierney's views have stood up well. No one has
challenged the fact that papal infallibility can be found nowhere in the
first millennium. At most it can be pushed back to the thirteenth century. Even after that date many disputed it, including Saint Thomas
More, who in the sixteenth century held that a general council was the
only way to solve the church's problems. From that time onwards—
especially in the struggles with Protestantism and Gallicanism—the
popes and many theologians slowly came to accept the doctrine of
papal infallibility. The classical formulation is by Saint Robert
Bellarmine (1542-1621) in the early seventeenth century, but there
were always strong objections to it, mainly but not exclusively, from
the Gallicans and Febronians. It was only in the nineteenth century

that an unchallenged notion of infallibility gained general acceptance. Francis A. Sullivan sensibly reminds us that while infallibility rates high in the estimation of many today (especially among reactionary Catholics) it is, in fact, a minor issue when seen within the context of the hierarchy of the truths of faith.[11] Hierarchy of truths is a traditional term that has become popular again as a result of Vatican II's Decree on Ecumenism which emphasized that dogmatic truths vary in their relationship "to the foundation of Christian faith." It is within this context that Sullivan emphasizes that Christian faith does not depend on papal infallibility.

THE ORDINARY MAGISTERIUM

Intimately linked with infallibility (sometimes called the "extraordinary magisterium") is the "ordinary and universal magisterium." There is a long church tradition of the Bishop of Rome taking a leadership role in sorting out doctrinal teaching.[12] Traditionally, this was normally done in consultation with the bishops rather than by the pope acting alone. The word "magisterium" refers to the teaching office of the church and the term "ordinary magisterium" refers to the pope's non-infallible, day-to-day teaching which, since Vatican I, is held to be binding in varying degrees on Catholics. However, it is also clear that despite the best will in the world, some may not be able to conscientiously to give assent to the ordinary magisterium. This does not in any way exclude them from the church. Part of the problem with the modern papacy is that since Vatican I, it has so much to say, and has spread its teaching authority into so many different areas that it has trivialized its own authority. Among some Catholics there is a kind of "magisteriolatry," or worship of the magisterium; Pius XII (1939-1958), for instance, literally pontificated on a vast range of topics.

The term "ordinary and universal magisterium" is of very recent origin and was first used in the other dogmatic constitution of Vatican I, *Dei Filius*.[13] It had been coined by the Jesuit theologian, Josef Kleutgen, who was one of the redactors of that document. It has subsequently come to be used as a catch-all phrase for papal teaching that has gradually taken on "quasi-infallible" status in popular perception. The addition of the word "universal" to the term "ordinary magisterium," indicates that a teaching is universally held by bishops and pope. Increasingly, especially during the Wojtyla papacy, the term "ordinary and universal magisterium" has been conflated with the infallible magisterium as though there were no distinctions between the two, and it tends to bestow on a teaching a status that it does not have. A teaching cannot be "quasi-infallible." Vatican I is clear: something is either infallible, or it is not; it has to belong to either the ordinary or the infallible magisterium.

PRIMACY IN THE FIRST MILLENNIUM

Unlike infallibility and ordinary magisterium, primacy has deep roots in church tradition.[14] But we must be careful not to approach the past looking for the present; the past must be treated within its own context. It is clear that the See of Rome was important from early in church history because it was the capital of the Roman Empire and it was there that the apostles Peter and Paul were martyred and buried. During the first three centuries of Christianity, Rome claimed leadership and this was generally recognized, but the pope had no practical way of imposing his will or views on the rest of the church. The church accepted that the leadership of Peter (and Paul) continued through the Roman bishop, who was seen as the center and focus of the unity of the churches. The ecclesiology of the early church focused on the local church, and its primal expression was the community gathered around the bishop celebrating the Eucharist. When the early church eventually came to think about a universal expression of itself, it was natural to say that just as the Eucharist was the primal bond of the local church, so a eucharistic nexus held all of the disparate local churches together in a universal unity. As the bishop gave expression to local eucharistic unity, so Peter's successor in Rome gave expression to universal eucharistic unity. The Roman bishop held the presidency of charity.

A connected idea is expressed by the Latin word *communio*. The universal church was thought of as an inter-communion of communions. Participation in Eucharistic Communion was an external sign of union with the church. The word "excommunication" referred to a denial of the Eucharist and thus to a severing of unity. Public sin led to personal excommunication, and the breakdown of unity between churches over issues of doctrine or discipline led bishops to excommunicate each other. Rome, as the center of ecclesial communion, was seen as the focus of unity; if you were in union with

Rome, you were in union with the church universal.

Rome was also, as Klaus Schatz calls it, "the privileged locus of tradition."[15] By this he means that Rome was viewed as the touchstone of orthodoxy and the Roman bishops had a broad sense of doctrinal responsibility for the whole church. But this does not mean that Rome dogmatically dominated the church. After the Emperor Constantine liberated Christianity from persecution in 312, the possibility of developing an "international church" with strong interconnections increased. The local church was still seen as the foundation but, following the Roman civil structure, these churches formed into provinces with a metropolitan bishop. The province was the focus of collegiality and it was the provincial bishops in synod, or the metropolitan, who approved the election of local bishops. Above this provincial organization were the patriarchical bishops of the principal churches—Rome, Alexandria, Antioch, and, after 325, Constantinople. Each of these had a "sphere of influence" (Rome's immediate sphere was central and southern Italy).

The problem, however, was that regional autonomy easily led to fractures in the universal church. The worst of these fractures mirrored the political and growing cultural split within the Empire itself: between the East (centered on Constantinople) and the West (politically centered in various places, but symbolized by Rome). Slowly, in the period between Popes Damasus I (366-384) and Gelasius I (492-496), Rome began to claim more and more authority. As the only patriarchate in the West, Rome was widely recognized as the center of ecclesial communion. Pope Damasus was the first to appeal directly to the Petrine text in Matthew (16:17-19) to support his position, and he claimed that his authority came not from the church but from the fact that he was Peter's successor. Siricus I (394-399) issued decretals responding to specific questions and it was his view that these had the force of law. The greatest pope of the period was Leo I (440-461). He envisaged the Bishop of Rome as having responsibility for the whole church. He intervened decisively at the Council of Chalcedon (451) and he held that the fidelity of Christ's commitment to Peter was eternal and that it found its contemporary realization in the actions of the Bishop of Rome.

Gelasius I also had high pretensions regarding the papacy and it was probably he who first asserted the superiority of the church over the state. In contrast to this it has to be said that, with the exception of the time of Leo I and Chalcedon, "the Roman church not only exercized no leadership in the East in normal times, but also that serious ecclesiastical divisions and conflicts could by no means be quickly resolved by appeals to Rome."[16]

While the actual split between eastern and western Christianity occurred in the Middle Ages, its origins go back to the late Roman Empire. However, even in the West there were real limits to the acceptance of papal jurisdiction. The practical problem was the collapse of centralized civil control after 407 with the barbarian incursions and the breakdown of the Roman communications system. But the important theological aspect was that Christians viewed the local community as the paradigm of the church, and the local bishop looked more to his fellow bishops in the local episcopal synod and to his metropolitan than he did to far-away Rome. One might appeal to Rome in a crisis, but that was a rare event. The Roman bishops claimed universal superintendence, but psychologically their practical horizon was confined to central Italy.

In an analysis of papal letters for the period of Gelasius I, Bernhard Schimmelpfennig shows that the popes' main area of influence was suburbicarian Italy. Beyond that there was only intermittent correspondence.[17] This is re-enforced by the *Liber Pontificalis* (a series of papal biographies) whose parochial focus gives a clue to the attitudes prevailing in the papal chancery.[18] It is largely centered on local ordinations and on the acquisition of property and ecclesiastical paraphernalia. In it there is no sense of the wider church. So, at the end of the first millennium, the pope's actual influence and power was confined to the *Patrimonium Petri*, the area immediately around Rome.[19] The pope was seen as the successor of Peter, the highest priest of Christendom and the touchstone of doctrinal truth. But he was a distant, almost mythical figure.

Perhaps it was better that people knew nothing about the reality, for many of the popes of the tenth century were completely depraved and the papacy had become the plaything of the Mafia-like feudal families of central Italy, of whom the Theophylact and Cresentii were the worst. This mirrored the situation throughout western Europe where local churches were controlled and owned by local feudal lords. The eastern half of Christendom was already practically divorced from Rome, with mutual ignorance and hostility.

PRIMACY IN THE SECOND MILLENNIUM

The papacy itself was reformed in the early eleventh century through the intervention of the German emperors. A series of popes, of whom the most important were Leo IX (1049-1054) and Gregory VII (1073-1085), initiated revolutionary changes by ridding the church of lay, feudal control of appointment to church offices (the investiture controversy), and by imposing universal celibacy on the western clergy. This led to a second stage of controversy between Rome (the key pope in this struggle was Innocent III [1198-1216]) and the Holy Roman Emperors about who was supreme in Christian society. The result was a gargantuan struggle that ultimately destroyed the Empire as a political entity and gave the papacy a Pyrrhic victory that eventually resulted in the popes leaving Rome for Avignon, and that also led to the Great Western Schism.[20] The medieval papacy adopted theocratic pretensions which today have still not been fully jettisoned. They have merely been shifted from the political sphere and refocused in the theological.

Church reform is always an ambivalent activity, for it is so easy to destroy the good when rooting out the evil. In the process of breaking lay and imperial control of the church and asserting the superiority of the spiritual, the medieval popes lost sight of the first millennium's emphasis on a Petrine theology of leadership and substituted a papal ideology of power. If the Greek word *diaconia* characterized papal leadership in the first millennium, the Latin word *potestas* characterized it in the second. Friedrich Heer argues that Catholicism is still living with the wedge driven between clergy and laity during the first stage of the medieval reform movement, and he suggests that the distinction between secular and sacred in European culture finds its origin in the struggle with the German emperors.[21] The same period also sees the origin of the idea of papal monarchy. But the irony is that while this period has been traversed thoroughly by historians and canonists, theologians have seemingly avoided it. During the Middle Ages there was hardly any serious ecclesiological reflection on the primatial claims of the popes. This is because the whole medieval debate was carried on in legal and canonical terms and was especially influenced by the renewal of Roman law. Medieval ecclesiology was extraordinarily weak.

The tension that we live with today is that, while our theology of the church is much stronger, it still has to co-exist with medieval legalistic notions of ecclesiastical polity that are fundamentally antagonistic to a more organic understanding of the church. This results in a corrosive disjunction that is far from being resolved. The most important of the great medieval popes was Innocent III. With him a truly hierocratic view of the papacy emerged. Hierocrats held that secular sovereignty was essentially derived from the church, and that the emperor or king was merely a vicar of the pope. For Innocent, power and the right to rule came directly from God. It did not come from below—from the church or the people. The pope was the mouthpiece of this divine inspiration.

The result of this hierocratic view was that the popes saw themselves as lords and kings of the world, holding the *plenitudo potestatis* ("the fullness of power," a concept derived from Roman law), and dispensing and withdrawing this power as political contingencies demanded. Some saw the papacy as the source of all power in the world. Although there is debate as to whether Innocent III saw himself this way, certainly Gregory IX (1227-1241) and Innocent IV (1243-1254) acted this way in their struggle with the German emperors, and the hierocratic view culminated in the absurdities of Boniface VIII (1294-1303) in his struggle with the French monarchy.

Canonical theorists after Innocent III pushed the hierocratic position to extreme lengths, and Boniface VIII argued in the bull *Unam sanctam* that the temporal is completely subject to the spiritual. Therefore, everyone must obey the pope and all temporal power and authority must be subject to the spiritual. The bull states clearly that obedience to the pope is a prerequisite for salvation. Lurking in these assertions is an interesting contemporary problem: is *Unam sanctam* infallible, or is it only ordinary magisterium? If it is neither of these, what is it? Various proposals have been put forward to solve this, but there is still no clear solution as to what we are to make doctrinally of Boniface's absurd claims.

The excesses of Boniface led directly to the move of the popes to Avignon (1309-1377). And Avignon led straight to the greatest crisis of papal history: the Great Western Schism. The schism broke in April 1378 with the first conclave in Rome in seventy-five years. It was surrounded by riot and controversy. It elected Urban VI (1378-1389), an unstable man of violent temper, who was possibly insane. In September, the cardinals declared they were not free in Urban's election and proceeded to elect Clement VII (1378-1394), who returned to Avignon.

There is a consensus among historians that Urban was elected under duress and that he was mentally unstable; the election of a person of unsound mind is illegal.[22] So after 1378 there were two doubtful popes. A series of Roman and Avignon popes were elected by their respective cardinals. The schism hardened into two irreconcilable camps: France, Spain, Portugal, and Scotland for the Avignon line; the rest of Europe for the Roman pope.

Thirty years later, in 1409, a third pope was elected by the Council of Pisa. It had met in an attempt to solve the schism, but it simply made the issue more complicated. The Council of Constance (1414-1418) was brought together by the emperor Sigismund to heal a schism that had now lasted for thirty-six years. Two ecclesiological theories, one oligarchic and the other democratic, underlay the Council. Both found their origin in the medieval notion of corporation. The oligarchic notion was that the cardinals formed a corporation or senate with the pope in the government of the church. Some canonists argued that the Roman church was constituted by pope and cardinals and that one could not act without the other. So when faced with a possibly insane pope, the cardinals felt they could stage an ecclesiastical coup d'état and depose Urban VI.

As the schism deepened, the more democratic tendency—represented by conciliarism—began to predominate. The key conciliar theorist was Cardinal Francesco Zabarella. He held that the whole mystical body of Christ was a corporation and that, as such, it could exercise jurisdiction especially when there was no head. Schism, he argued, created a quasi-vacancy in the papacy since neither claimant could govern the whole church. In these circumstances the authority of the church should be exercised by the *congregatio fidelium* ("congregation of the faithful") gathered in general council. Zabarella held that the Council's authority came, not from who convoked it, but from the whole body of Christ.

Most historians now accept that Constance was ecumenical from the beginning, despite the lack of papal convocation. An older school held that it was "ecumenical" only after 4 July 1415 when the legate of the Roman pope, Gregory XII, staged a rereading of the bull of convocation. The Council itself, having declared the papacy vacant, ran the church for three years. Eventually Martin V (1417-1431) was elected by a college chosen by the Council. The key document of Constance is the decree *Haec sancta*, which says that the Council represents the whole church and that its power comes "immediately from Christ."[23] It further taught that everyone in the church, even the pope, was "bound to obey it." Ultimately, what is asserted is the superiority of a general council over the pope.

Constance also decreed that councils be held at regular intervals, but once the schism was healed the conciliar movement petered out fairly quickly. The fifteenth-century popes continued to act as petty Italian princelings and, while there was considerable cultural achievement during the Renaissance in Rome, the late fifteenth and early sixteenth centuries were a time of ecclesiastical disaster. It led to the religious revolution initiated by Luther.

With the coming of the Reformation there was a rapid retreat from conciliarist positions and an increasing stress on notions of papal primacy derived from the political model of absolute monarchy. As in the case of infallibility, it was Bellarmine in the early seventeenth century who gave expression to the idea of primacy which was taken up by Vatican I. No one can take away or diminish the power of the supreme pontiff, not the college of cardinals, nor a general council, nor the pope himself, because papal authority comes immediately from God and is not subject to the control of any created will.[24] Substantially this is the contemporary position. But the question remains: how traditional is this teaching and how acceptable would it have been in the first millennium?

There is a second question that emerges from *Haec sancta*. Today we see primacy through the prism of the definition of Vatican I. But Vatican I ignored *Haec sancta* by presupposing that it was not a genuine conciliar definition. That, however, is a view that is no longer tenable. So how can primacy, as defined at Vatican I, be reconciled with Constance? Some theologians get around this by moving the discussion forward to Vatican II and claiming that this council redresses the imbalance of papal centralism. But the fact is that Vatican II does not set any limits to papal power either; it simply speaks of the relationship of the bishops to the pope, acknowledging what had been effectively forgotten: that bishops are members of the apostolic college with ordinary authority that flows essentially from their office.

Vatican II is also hard to reconcile with Constance when it says: "A council is never ecumenical unless it is confirmed or at least accepted as such by the successor of Peter."[25] In other words, neither Vatican I nor Vatican II dealt with the teaching of Constance that an ecumenical council is superior to any pope. All of these questions still remain to be answered.

Despite this, the Wojtyla papacy has ironically brought to realization, in the last years of the second Christian millennium, the notion of high ecclesiastical power that several of the popes of the last thousand years have claimed as their own. However, during this second millennium of church history, the theoretical assertion of papal power always coexisted with effective inhibitions from ecclesiastical and civil structures, and alternative views of church polity that limited the expression of papal power and prevented over-centralization. The sheer difficulty of communication and the impossibility of enforcing papal directions in the pre-modern era acted as an effective inhibiter of Romanization.

Nowadays these checks and balances have disappeared, and the popular perception that the pope equals the church, while not theologically correct nor true to tradition, represents the reality of what is actually happening. Certainly, episcopal collegiality, ecumenical councils, the doctrine of reception, and an enhanced sense of lay dignity still theoretically exist as a potential check on power, but it is the papacy that totally controls the structures through which these checks and balances operate.

In the last twenty years these Vatican II doctrines have not been taken seriously. It is for this reason that I have claimed that the Wojtyla papacy is the most powerful in history. However, a caveat needs to be added to that assertion: with the abolition of the Roman Inquisition and an inability to call in the secular authorities to enforce papal decrees, it is more difficult now to enforce the papal will. As a result, increasingly severe ecclesiastical penalties are being invoked: for example, the excommunication of the Sri Lankan theologian, Father Tissa Balasuriya. Also an increasingly theologically sophisticated laity is quite unmoved by ecclesiastical fulminations.

THE DOCTRINE OF RECEPTION

Faith in Christ and his teaching is a free act and can never be forced. One receives the word of God and accepts Jesus as the one whom God has sent. The same principle can be applied to the Christian community; it too must give consent to doctrinal teaching. Thus, in the early church, acceptance of episcopal or conciliar teaching was confirmed as part of the apostolic tradition by the agreement and consensus of the local churches. However, as in the case of the Arian heresy, it often took considerable time for conciliar teaching to be finally received by the large majority of faithful Christians. Sadly, this traditional notion of reception came to be obscured by the ideology of obedience that dominated the latter part of the second millennium of church history. But since Vatican II, the traditional notion of reception by the *congregatio fidelium* is regaining theological currency.

What is reception? Essentially, it is a confirmation and acceptance into Christian consciousness that a decision or teaching of the magisterium is believable and/or livable. Sullivan says that "subsequent reception does not confer infallibility on the act of the magisterium," but it bestows upon the decision the certainty "that an infallible definition has taken place."[26] In other words, there is a subtle distinction between the Gallican position—that a teaching gained infallible status only if it was subsequently accepted by the church—and the contemporary position, that acceptance confirms that the teaching was infallible in the first place.

But what happens when the church does not receive a teaching, such as the teaching of Paul VI on contraception? While this was not proposed as infallible teaching, it is now being put forward by the Vatican as an exercise of the "universal ordinary magisterium." But it has not been received by the vast majority of Catholics of fertile age, other Catholics, and many clergy, let alone other Christians. So we have to say at this point that this teaching has simply not been received and, as such, cannot be construed as the teaching of the church.

Increasingly, I think, the norm of reception will be applied to a whole range of church teachings, particularly in the areas of church authority and personal sexuality.

THE FUTURE OF THE PAPACY

What can we draw from tradition to help us into the future? Firstly, we need to reassert the church's synodal tradition. The church is not an absolute monarchy. While it is not a democracy either, its essential structure has much more in common with a democratic model than an imperial one.[27] It is built upon the local community, and in our culture this is more likely to be expressed by people with common interests or common bonds than by a strictly geographical unit such as a parish. This community should be the primary locus of decision-making. Local communities gather in dioceses, which, nowadays, need to be much smaller units; my view is that there ought to be at least one bishop for every 100,000 Catholics. At present there are about 2,500 dioceses with 965 million Catholics.[28] To achieve my ideal, there would have to be three to four times the present number of dioceses. Leadership at both the local and diocesan level should be elected. Diocesan bishops, and representative priests and laity, would form the national synod and the elected president of that synod would act as metropolitan. If the Bishop of Rome is to continue to exercise a truly international role in the church, he ought to be elected by a college made up of the metropolitans together with representatives of clergy, religious and laity. Leonard Swidler has already published a detailed proposal for the development of a Catholic constitution.[29]

Secondly, we need a new general council rather than an ecumenical council. A general council (like the councils of the second millennium) represents the western Roman Catholic Church; an ecumenical council is much broader and includes the representatives of the other Christian churches. The Orthodox churches hold (correctly, in my view) that a truly ecumenical council will be impossible as long as the church remains split. If, as the Council of Constance mandated, there were regular decennial general councils, these could gradually move toward a true ecumenical council with the increasingly full participation of the Orthodox, Protestants, and Anglicans.

What the Roman Catholic Church needs immediately is a general council, but the last thing we need is Vatican III! The next council should be held as far away from Rome and the Vatican as possible in order to protect it from the machinations of the Vatican curia. It would need to be organized and run by a body representing the world episcopate under the presidency of the pope. It would deal with problems such as the crisis in the priesthood and ministry, the complex ethical and social issues facing modern society, and the need to reinterpret the meaning structures that underpin our culture. It would also have to confront the crisis of authority by rethinking and re-contextualizing the Vatican I definitions, especially on primacy and magisterium.

There is, in addition, a real need to recover the various levels of magisterial teaching: the conciliar magisterium, the episcopal magisterium, and the theological magisterium. Coterminous with this would be the recovery of the doctrine of reception by the *congregatio fidelium*.

This council would also need to deal decisively with the Roman Curia. This anachronistic, baroque institution (in its present form it comes from the early sixteenth century) has no place in the modern world. It ought to be replaced by a much smaller secretariat staffed by competent Catholics who actually represent the broader church, rather than the narrowly scholastic, ministerially inexperienced, and unrepresentative staff of the contemporary Vatican.

In other words, I am suggesting that, just as the church at the beginning of the second millennium was revolutionized to face a new and challenging medieval world, so as it enters the third Christian millennium it must face an even more radical change. If it fails in this, its future will be very problematic indeed.

Notes

1. For a fuller development of all this see my *Papal Power: A Proposal for Change in Catholicism's Third Millennium* (London: Harper Collins, 1997).

2. For Latin and English texts see Norman P. Tanner, ed., *Decrees of the Ecumenical Councils*, vol. II (London: Sheed and Ward, 1990), pp. 811ff.

3. Ibid., p. 816.

4. Francis A. Sullivan, *Magisterium: Teaching Authority in the Catholic Church* (New York: Paulist Press, 1983). See esp. pp. 99ff.

5. Tanner, *Decrees of the Ecumenical Councils*, vol. II, p. 813.

6. Ibid., pp. 813-814.

7. Ibid., p. 814.

8. Cuthbert Butler, *The Vatican Council*, 1869-1870 (London: Collins, 1930). Reprinted 1962, p. 332. For the primacy debate see pp. 330-347. This still remains the best general work in English on Vatican I.

9. Ibid.

10. Brian Tierney, *Origins of Papal Infallibility, 1150-1350: A Study on the Concepts of Infallibility, Sovereignty, and Tradition in the Middle Ages* (Leiden: E.J. Brill, 1972).

11. Sullivan, *Magisterium*, p. 117.

12. Ibid., pp. 63-78.

13. Tanner, *Decrees of the Ecumenical Councils,* vol. II, p. 807. For a history of the term see John P. Boyle, "The Ordinary Magisterium," *Heythrop Journal*, 20 (1979), pp. 380-398 and 21 (1980), pp. 14-29. See also, Sullivan, *Magisterium*, pp. 122ff.

14. See my treatment of this whole period in Collins, op. cit., pp 130-155.

15. Klaus Schatz, *Papal Primacy. From Its Origins to the Present*, English trans., (Collegeville: The Liturgical Press, 1996), pp. 7-28.

16. Ibid., p. 27.

17. Bernhard Schimmelpfennig, *The Papacy*, English trans. (New York: Columbia University Press, 1992), p. 50.

18. For an English translation see Raymond Davis, *The Book of Pontiffs* (Liverpool: Liverpool University Press), 2 vols., 1989 and 1992.

19. For the tenth century see Gerd Tellenbach, *The Church in Western Europe from the Tenth to the Early Twelfth Century* (Cambridge: Cambridge University Press), 1993, pp. 65-74.

20. There is a vast historiographic literature on this period. See the works of Walter Ullmann and Brian Tierney's *The Crisis of Church and State, 1050-1300* (Toronto: University of Toronto Press, 1988), and Geoffrey Barraclough, *The Medieval Papacy* (London: Thames and Hudson, 1968).

21. Friedrich Heer, *The Medieval World; Europe from 1100 to 1350* (London: Weidenfeld and Nicholson, English trans., 1962), pp. 323-325.

22. See August Franzen, "The Council of Constance: Present State of the Problem," *Concilium*, VII, p. 19.

23. For *Haec sancta* see Tanner, vol. I, pp. 409-410.

24. Bellarmine quoted in James Brodrick, *Robert Bellarmine: Saint and Scholar* (London: Burns & Oates, 1961), p. 257.

25. *Lumen gentium*, 3, 22. Walter M. Abbott, ed., *The Documents of Vatican II* (New York: Guild Press, 1966), p. 157.

26. Sullivan, *Magisterium,* p. 111.

27. Eugene C. Bianchi and Rosemary Radford Ruether, eds., *A Democratic Catholic Church: The Reconstruction of Catholicism* (New York: Crossroad, 1992).

28. Felician A. Foy and Rose M. Avato, *1996 Catholic Almanac* (Huntington, In.: Our Sunday Visitor, 1996), p. 368.

29. Leonard Swidler, *Toward a Catholic Constitution* (New York: Crossroad, 1996).

4

A Spiritual Papacy

GIANCARLO ZIZOLA

In every part of the world, Catholics—and not only Catholics—are wondering out loud who will succeed John Paul II in the primatial See of Rome. It is a question that easily leads to another. Will a new pope mean reform of the papacy?

This second question was being asked already in the final months of the pontificate of Paul VI, but in an abstract and occasional way. The significant new fact today is that the two issues—that of the successor and that of the search for a new model of papacy more in keeping with the needs of the highest office in the church—are being formulated as organically and indivisibly linked. In other words, the option for or against reform of the papacy has become one of the factors in the choice of candidates and in the formulation of the qualifying platforms being drawn up by the representatives of different tendencies within the college of cardinals.

It might be argued that there is some significant probability that, in the nature of things, the same connection would be made on the occasion of every papal election. It should be recognized, nevertheless, that an active role in the establishment of this linkage today was played by John Paul's decision in May 1995 to insert in the order of the day of the Catholic church, and of ecumenical relations, "the search for a manner of exercising the primacy that would be open to a new situation" (to quote his words in the encyclical *Ut unum sint* ["That They May Be One"]).

Even though the results of that letter were not particularly satisfactory, at least within the ecumenical discussion, it is nevertheless possible to discern in it a number of critical elements, in the etymological sense of the Greek root—*crisis*—which implies a just judgment on the past. These elements can be used to direct the discussion of papal reform on a less abstract path than in the past. By virtue of that initiative, the See of Peter has formulated the decision to accept responsibility for the project of the new model of papacy and its implementation. It is undertaking papal reform as an item of ordinary business in spite of the fact that this is an issue so delicate and so loaded with explosive tensions as to require in earlier centuries the intervention of the Ecumenical Council—the only body judged to have the power to bind the papacy to its own reform. Without committing himself to the calls—however authoritative—made known within the Catholic church in favor of a new universal council, the Slav pope has decided to pledge himself to undertake what might be called a refounding phase of his office, in dialogue with other Christian churches. Evidently he has taken into account all the advantages of being able to determine the conditions and the limits of an acceptable reform project.

It should also be noted, however, that a reform of this kind could only emerge from within, that is to say, from the spiritual currents in the church itself, along with theological reflections and the advice of sister churches. John Paul has believed that only "offering itself with the humiliations to the inspirations," as Pascal said, could the papacy lift itself out of the crisis in which it is plunged on the temporal level and break down the barriers between the various sheepfolds of Christ. Only thus could it become such a point of concentration of spiritual authority in the eyes of all Christians and of all peoples as to become a kind of agent of unification of all the forces that tend toward the good, without losing at the same time continuity with what had previously been considered good.

The insertion of the question of the future model of the papacy in the order of the day of the debate has resulted immediately in raising the level of the customary pre-election discussions in the Roman church. It has made it clear that the task at hand is not simply to identify the suitable candidates, the *papabili*, but also to define the nature of a spiritual office that is of direct concern to almost a billion Catholics, an office that additionally affects the process of reunion of divided Christians, as well as dialogue among the great religions of the world and even the political governments of the world system.

The structural form of the debate surrounding the selection of the new pope has produced a further expansion of public interest, both in the church and in society, regarding the programmatic question of reform of the papacy. A theme that is normally reserved to the power brokers and the cardinals might consequently be said to have become "democratized," demonstrating that a public opinion in the church can be developed legitimately and in a manner beneficial to the community, without degenerating necessarily into "pressure groups" or into attempts to manipulate the electors.

As a matter of fact, a lively discussion has been started at all levels in the church. Examples are: the interdisciplinary symposium organized by the Congregation for the Doctrine of the Faith in December 1996 on "The Primacy of the Successor of Peter," a symposium in which three representatives of the other Christian confessions participated; the public interventions of Cardinals Joseph Ratzinger and Godfried Danneels; the remarkable conference given at Oxford in June 1996 by retired Archbishop of San Francisco John Quinn;[1] the essay on primacy published by Father Klaus Schatz, S.J.; and the many contributions provided by analysts of the Vatican situation that focused specifically on the problems of succession to John Paul II. This multiple production can be seen not only as an effective exercise of the "sense of faith" which the Vatican Council recognized as existing in the *universitas fidelium* ("the body of the faithful as a whole"),[2] but also formulated in the 1996 Apostolic Constitution, *Universi Dominici Gregis*, of John Paul II, which said that the election of a pope "is not an event isolated from the People of God and of concern only to the electoral college, but in a certain sense an action of the entire church."

The development, on the ecumenical level and within the Roman church itself, of a public culture favorable to reform of the papacy allows us to hope that a program of this kind will not end up by falling prisoner to the logic of the power holders, or, worse still, be suffocated by the interests of the Roman curia. At the same time we have to keep in mind that the history of papal reform is overwhelmingly the history of failure, from the human point of view, and that reforms have been effected through violent political upsets and under the pressures of deep religious tensions rather than through consensual programs.

What would seem necessary to establish as a starting condition, if this new reform program is not to end up as an illusion, is that it would be difficult for any *aggiornamento* in this strategic field to succeed by the application of measures that are only limited and superficial. It is a matter of record that the exercise of the Petrine office in the See of Rome has known different paradigms and forms throughout the centuries. In the second millennium the papacy underwent a process of extreme centralization which altered the paradigm that had characterized the first millennium. While presented as an institution symbolizing social stability and a pillar of public order and of conservatism, the papacy was in fact the object of modifications resulting from the evolution of the forms of sovereignty in the civil field. Its historical experience cannot therefore exclude the possibility of the papacy assuming once more a functional form different from what we have known up to this time, reworking and synthesizing the elements of flexibility that have already distinguished the models offered in the second half of the twentieth century by Pius XII, John XXIII, Paul VI, and John Paul II.

While deserving our full attention, this "minimalist" attempt at reform (as one might call it) does not seem to have won a general consensus among theologians. For this kind of evaluation of the primacy, John Paul's encyclical has legitimized the method of distinguishing the unchangeable substance of the dogma of papal primacy and the historically established and variable concrete forms in which it has been expressed. This way of looking at the issue may produce useful demythifying elements, but it runs the risk of consigning to the trash can of reform nothing more than a few accessories, reducing reform to a kind of window dressing, and thereby ensuring the better performance of the traditional machine.

Taking this possibility into account, the comment of Pierre Vallin seems justifiable. The work of reform of the papacy, he says, cannot avoid being related to the evolution of dogma, an evolution that may not be excluded in this field too, if we hope to reach a contemporary definition of the foundations and the functions of a primacy of the church of Rome. "It is possible to anticipate in this light," the Jesuit of the Sevres Center in Paris has written, "that historical and theological studies carried out in common with the other ecclesial traditions will lead, in years to come, to a renewed understanding of what is really tied to the confession of faith in the Western church's perception of a universal primacy of the bishop of Rome. The simple distinction between the dogmatic foundation, which goes back to a divine institution, and the ways in which the primacy is exercised (ways that alone would be subject to error, dysfunction or blunders) cannot be regarded as adequate in the situation of Christian faith in our times. The voice of all Christians, of all the churches, should be listened to seriously and modestly. It is our conviction that a raising of theological consciousness regarding the relativity of the doctrinal formulations of a given epoch and a given cultural ambience, can one day develop a process that in due course would lift itself to the level of a dogmatic conscience worked out in interecclesial processes of reception and recognition."[3]

In addition to deeper theological understanding, one of the prime elements needed in the execution of this kind of reform is water from the spiritual well. The principal objective of such reform is to increase the influence of the papacy as a spiritual authority respectful of all kinds of diversity. It follows that its purification from the trappings of time can be the result of facing up more realistically to the demands of the New Testament and to collective spiritual processes modeled on what occurred in the primitive church of Jerusalem during the incarceration of Peter when "they prayed to God for him unremittingly."[4]

The reference to the development of the charismatic reality of the church is intended to provide the critical material that is indispensable from the moment when reform can no longer avoid affecting the political system of the papacy and the forms that have grown out of the osmosis with absolutist regimes. Contemporary ways of thinking that have moved in the direction of democratic, parliamentary, and popular political structures, do not tolerate forms and methods of action that are seen, rightly or wrongly, as smelling of authoritarianism or a cult of personality.

For a reform of that scope and complexity, however, it would be a mistake to imagine that all that would be needed would be to bring the papacy into line with a more modern secular model, even if the church, in order to be a communion, would need to be more than a democracy and not less. A glance at the history of the church should make it clear to us that a political weakening of the papal system (which represents a reasonable objective for the full spiritual expansion of what its function should be in the next century) can only be achieved in the context of a symmetrical spiritual strengthening. It is not accidental or exceptional that criticism of legal centralism in the church and of the dizzy pretensions of papal control and temporal power has always been expressed principally by men and women of the cloister, such people as Saint Bernard of Clairvaux, Saint Peter Damien, and Saint Catherine of Siena.

This kind of criticism is no less needed today than it was in the time of Eugene III, Innocent III, and Boniface VIII, even if it has to be reformulated in the light of the current needs of the church. On the threshold of the third millennium, the question of the papacy must be redefined as a dependent variable of the broader question of Christianity, and of Christianity placed in the context of post-modern society. Unless we analyze with sufficient clarity the course of the crisis of Christianity in the twentieth century and the limits of the strategies of containment adopted by the Roman church, we will have difficulty in dealing dispassionately with the evolution that can be anticipated in the near future.

The Christian mission has obviously entered a confused, disturbing, and tragic phase as we near the end of the "short century." The strategy adopted by the church during that century was based essentially on the expectation—a mixture of self-deceiving over-confidence, presumption, and mistaken analyses—that the cultural and social framework could hold up against the most massive attacks of the models of life presented everywhere by the market economy and industrialization.

Such was the expectation that underlay the church's decision in the second half of the twentieth century to work to restore "a Christian society" by means of new formulas and mechanisms. This project was implemented not only in concordats and in the Christian Democratic political parties, but also in the social teaching of the church—Jacques Maritain's anti-integralist theory—and above all in the effort of complex ecclesiological rethinking undertaken at the Second Vatican Council in the 1960s. All these initiatives constituted an enormous spiritual, intellectual, and political effort of the church to produce the most valid reply possible—no longer bunkered behind the walls of the sacred but in the midst of society itself—to the challenge of secularization in its twofold form: liberalist and communist.

Once the phase of institutional reforms—as defined by a conservative interpretation of the directives of Vatican II—had been completed, the strategy of "the new Christian society" was resumed and pursued with exceptionally dynamic commitment by John Paul II. Under his pontificate, the church has presented itself once again, under the guise of an updating, as a *societas perfecta inequalis* ("unequal perfect society"), committing itself to the systematic exercise of an ethico-political role in the center of modern society, and taking full advantage of the crisis of that society. The papacy has taken its seat among the contemporary powers, expanding its presence in international organizations, in relations with other states, and in the world system of the communications media. The diplomatic possibilities deriving from the international status of the Holy See have reached the highest possible level, with the development of the system of nunciatures, the recovery of the legal and property assets that had existed before the communist system in East-Central Europe, and organic recourse to the instrument of concordats. The spiritual primacy of the papacy has in this way clothed itself in and become confused with a neo-medieval re-edition of a political primacy among the nations, thereby inescapably obscuring the pastoral qualifications appropriate to the functions of the bishop of Rome.

The many temptations and difficulties to which the functioning of this system is exposed constitute a problem that has been obvious for some time in the church. It is recognized that the existence of an apparatus similar to that of temporal sovereignty has undeniable benefits. It helps, in particular, to develop a planetary awareness that is more disposed to consider such questions as religious freedom, international economic justice, the interests of humanity, and the importance of bioethics. The self-defensive reaction of the Holy See to the almost total defeat of Catholic political parties would seem to have resulted from the papacy's anxiety to acquire its own autonomous and efficient political and diplomatic system. There remain nevertheless counterindications that were pointed out by Father Vallin when he noted that "an important revision will be necessary in the course of the next decades, in particular, to create a more meaningful distinction between the function of an international organization that has resulted from a particular limited history (the United Nations) and the properly universal primacy in relation to the Catholic churches that belongs to the church of Rome—the church in which is venerated the memory of the martyrs, of Saint Peter and of Saint Paul."[5]

When we take the ecumenical priorities into account, we can see that getting rid of the papal politico-diplomatic apparatus is an issue that needs to be urgently faced, since the Holy See's political role cannot be counted among the essential prerogatives of the pope's mission.

No pope, as Olivier Clément has noted, was head of a state during the first eight centuries of Christianity, and "it is by no means essential to the exercise of the primacy that the bishop of Rome name the bishops of the entire world; or that he have his own see on a sovereign territory and be a Head of State among all those powerful ones who call themselves 'benefactors'; and that he should, in consequence, have diplomatic representatives."[6] It is obvious that this political arrangement represents a disparity, a lack of symmetry between the Roman Catholic Church and the other Christian churches and communities. These latter bodies may indeed have forms of international collaboration, but they do not enjoy—nor do they seek to enjoy—a similar sociopolitical international presence.

Doubts and questionings are to be found even among Catholics. Not a few are convinced that the Holy See could be at least equally effective if it forewent the forms of state diplomacy and the structures of political sovereignty in its interventions, adopting instead the status of a non-governmental international organization (NGO), with functions and immunities similar to those enjoyed by UNESCO. Some objections were raised already during the Second Vatican Council. The Holy See, it was said, should not have a diplomatic corps nor should it exercise diplomatic functions, because these were instruments of political power and of worldly influence, whereas the church—by reason of its essentially religious nature—neither has, nor should have, a specific political function. The critics at the Council also stressed the danger that the Holy See would be seen as a state like other states and, accordingly, as a political power on a par with other state powers; and further, that it might compromise itself and indeed be forced to compromise itself, with the policies of states that were not always honest but even at times criminal.

Paul VI, in response to such requests, tried to reform the system by means of the Apostolic Letter *Sollicitudo omnium ecclesiarum* (1969). It identified the papal representatives as having a primarily ecclesial function, that of "making the bonds of unity between the Apostolic See and the local churches more solid." The priority of the ecclesial objectives of communion between the pope and the bishops over political objectives was reaffirmed by the Code of Canon Law.[7] In addition, the Vatican has developed an international activity that is more and more centered on the universal ethical magisterium (the right to life, for example, and the social rights of the family as such) rather than on specific political interventions. The international activities of the Holy See have always focused more on the interests of the universal common good than on issues of bilateral relations between states, a fact that provides some prospect of an evolution going beyond the political system that makes the pope a head of state, even if the number of states accredited to the Holy See has grown in less than a hundred years from 4, under Leo XIII, to 165, under John Paul II.

Among the undesirable effects of the reassertion—and indeed of the strengthening—of the Vatican's political and diplomatic system, is one often stressed; namely, an objectively harmful compromise of the papacy with worldly powers. This is particularly damaging to the Christian testimony of an institution whose principal way of identifying itself and of announcing the gospel, should rest on total commitment to God, and not on earthly powers. The danger exists of a crystallization on the papacy of an image of sovereignty that, in spite of pastoral adaptations, still resonates with its own historic debts to the ideology of ancient absolutist states.

The historic origins of the transfer from the realm of the state to that of the church—at the beginning of the modern era—of the concept of sovereignty that had been developed in the period of political absolutism, are well known. With the help of reactionary ideologues—the best known of whom was Joseph De Maistre, author of *Du Pape* ("about the Pope")—the church defined itself as a *societas perfecta* on the same level as the sovereign state, with a sovereign head—the pope. The intent of this action was to protect the church's autonomy vis-à-vis the state. The jurisdictional primacy of the pope and his dogmatic infallibility (to which De Maistre added the concept of political and state sovereignty) provided the legitimation, both theological and legal, of this internal and external sovereignty.

The understanding of papal primacy and infallibility in the framework of the concept of absolute sovereignty played a progressively bigger role in theological thinking as the nineteenth century approached its end. The primacy was more and more presented as the jurisdiction that determined everything, in every part of the church, and infallibility was seen as the unconditional affirmation of authority, far beyond the limitations established by the First Vatican Council. Although political retrenchment among the states of Europe had been brought to an end much earlier by the revolutions of 1830, Gregory XVI and Pius IX remained steadfast in their convictions. Their ecclesiology not only committed itself to the further strengthening of papal authority, but it "understood all of Christianity and the church in general as a *sistema auctoritatis* ('system of authority'). And that authority was understood above all as formal and legal authority, as *potestas* ('power'), in a word, as the sovereign decision-making power of the pope. This authority did not have to be legitimized by its contents. Instead, it is formal, resting on divine authorization. And all of this to ensure the unity and the self-sufficiency of the church, as these were then understood."[8]

The results of this kind of contamination of the theological level of the primacy by political lordship, and of the papacy understood as a pastoral mission by the papacy understood as a state, have not yet been fully eliminated from Catholic culture. A recent editorial in *La civiltà cattolica*, the magazine of the Italian Jesuits, has deplored this fact: "The superimposing of these elements—perhaps at times with the connivance of some church opinion makers—has meant that the pope continues to be erroneously regarded by large parts of public and church opinion as the holder of extensive political, financial, and—more generally—temporal power; from the concept of the pope as sovereign there follows a curious formulation of titles, of ceremonial behaviors, and above all of mentality which, in spite of the reform on this subject attempted by Paul VI, still survives, and not always with obvious benefit for Christian authenticity."[9]

To this same inherited sickness of sovereignty, aggravated since the dogmatic proclamations of 1870, is to be attributed the so-called "infallibilism" that confuses infallibility with impeccability. What we have here, according to *La civiltà cattolica*, is "a psycho-sociological attitude, not always free of servility, typical in a way of the court mentality that springs up, outside the pure doctrine of the personal infallibility of the pope, as an abnormal growth on that doctrine; and if, perhaps for secondary reasons, it has been possible to develop an apologetic rationale, let it be said frankly that this has been the effect and the cause of that ecclesiastical pyramid-building that has seen a proliferation of papolatry and courtly Byzantinism."

There exists, consequently, in the Catholic church a quite consistent (even if not yet theologically decisive) current of opinion that challenges the papacy to clarify the dogmatic definitions of 1870 by a courageous effort to contextualize these definitions within the cultural and political framework of that period of the history of the western church. The question of the development of papal absolutism, in the forms in which the editorial of *La civiltà cattolica* have sketched it, needs in turn to be placed in historical context if we are not to fall into the ingenuousness of the maximalists for whom the same could happen today as happened at the time of *Unam sanctam*. But it is difficult to deny that evils do occur in the church because of the cryptostatal forms in which the problem of power is presented within it, even if in sublimated form. Also assuming—even if only as a hypothesis—Klaus Schatz's viewpoint, according to which the jurisdictional overlay that has accumulated on the concrete structure of papal primacy may perhaps be "the necessary price to pay in order to obtain a substantially spiritual value," we still have to ask ourselves whether procedures exist in the church that constitute effective counterweights against possible abuses, as well as adequate remedies for what this German historian calls "the blind alleys inherent in the system." The urge to self-defense of papal authority and the self-referring recourse to the sole papal magisterium—considered to be unchangeable—have revealed all their dangerous qualities in the obstinacy with which the papacy has trapped itself in those blind alleys in its encounter with liberalism and during the Modernist crisis at the beginning of the twentieth century.

From the biblical and theological point of view these behaviors have revealed the constant risk to which Peter is exposed, of exchanging the messianic dignity and the divine filiation of Jesus, which he had proclaimed before the others, for a sharing of earthly power, ending up as a result by being rejected as Satan.[10] "As long as this theme, which is not simply the generic issue of the 'errors' of the 'non-infallible' magisterium, has not been developed in the theology of the primacy," Father Schatz has stressed, "the real history also will be only partially developed."

Schatz has also proposed some forms of juridically guaranteed reservation of certain issues to intermediate bodies in the ecclesiastical organization (national episcopal conferences and continental councils), with the Roman center committing itself not to intervene, or to intervene only in clearly defined situations, by analogy with the plurality and autonomy of these centers in early Christianity and with the structure of the patriarchates. In an ecclesiological essay published in Germany in 1969, Joseph Ratzinger himself has made the same proposal as useful for remodelling relations between the papal primacy and the churches.[11]

Another suggestion of Schatz concerns the validity of the decree *Haec sancta* issued by the Council of Constance, 6 April 1415, to deal with—beyond the specific emergency of that moment (the Western Schism)—extreme situations of a breakdown of the papacy, for example, a new papal schism, a "heretical pope," a pope who preys on the church through simony, or a pope who is losing his mind. All these hypothetical cases were discussed unemotionally by the medieval theologians and canonists, whereas at the present time, because the church has resigned itself to a self-deluding interpretation of papal sovereignty, it is almost unable from the juridical point of view to deal with similar eventualities.

Should the case occur—and it is not excluded by any grace of state—that a pope is no longer *compos sui* ("of sound mind"), Father Schatz notes, "a serious structural crisis would result in the church today. This is true also, and even more emphatically, for the preceding 'grey zone' of reduced psychic capacity and nervous resistance." From this follows the need to accept as a model to regulate the church's "right of resistance" the decree issued by the Council of Constance to deal with a particular situation. That would permit the calling of an authorized and authoritative ecumenical council, even without the presence of a papal subject who had become obviously unable to carry out the duties of the office validly.[12]

Furthermore, the required critique of the abusive contamination of the papal primacy by political sovereignty includes, for the great majority of the authors who have dealt with this issue in recent times, the need to develop in the Catholic church a higher level of synodal culture. If we want to ensure that the constitution of the church not be totally "absolutistic" on the level of constitutional law, it is clear that the statute of the Synod of Bishops has to be reformulated in ways that will ensure a better participation of the bishops in the exercise of the primacy. Cardinal Danneels, archbishop primate of Malines-Brussels, has called for a "council of the crown" around the pope, to consist of six or seven cardinals from around the world who would function as counselors.

What this and similar proposals seek to emphasize is that the church was established by Christ simultaneously "on the foundation of Peter" and "on the foundation of the apostles." They are also a reaction to the tendency of the Roman curia to downplay a true episcopal collegiality in the government of the church, stressing that episcopal collegiality should also always be a "critical and limiting" element, able to accept conflict courageously, and also recognizing the duty to correct vis-à-vis the pope. Peter, according to the gospel, was, in fact, given the task of strengthening the brethren once he himself had recovered.[13]

In some of the discussions of this issue, strong doubts have been expressed as to whether the inherited form of absolute monarchy is compatible, without risk of abuse of power, with what the Petrine function has become with the most recent developments of the Roman church. It is possible to fear that Peter might become a stumbling block not only for the other Christian churches but also for himself, if the actual structure were to be retained without prudent and, indeed, daring modifications.

If all the cards are put on the table, the conclusion has to be that the papacy has become a position that cannot be filled by a single person. The absolutism of the pope's dogmatic status is precisely the main cause of the fact that this situation is unsustainable.

When the First Vatican Council formulated the dogmas of papal primacy and infallibility, the bishops present in the hall were 774 out of about a thousand active bishops in the whole Catholic church. According to the 1997 *Annuario Pontificio*, the Catholic bishops today in office number some 4,600. Those retired, about a thousand, are more numerous than the Fathers at Pius IX's council. At the end of the nineteenth century, the Catholics who feared for the freedom of that pope, who had just been despoiled of his kingdom, numbered 272 million, most of them in Europe. Now Catholics number nearly a billion, the majority of them in Africa, Latin America, and Asia. By the end of this century, on the basis of current projections, nearly three of every four Catholics will live in what we have come to call the South, while their church will continue to function according to theological and canonical paradigms that are predominantly Eurocentric.

At the start of the century a dozen countries had ambassadors accredited to the Holy See. As it ends, there are one hundred eighty. The person who was the head and sovereign of the principal Christian church has become a world religious leader whose duties include ecumenical, interreligious, diplomatic, theological, pastoral, and political activities—all of them on a global scale.

The question that leaps to the mind is whether the papal institution has not become so unsupportable as to be sacrificial. We have the example of Pope Luciani (John Paul I) whose reign lasted a mere thirty-three days, and now the "pyramidal syndrome" that has struck the psychophysical colossus that was Pope Wojtyla (John Paul II) in a context in which we cannot exclude with certainty that his brain problems are not traceable to the pyramidal structure of his office and to the stress created by this kind of sovereignty.

If there is a probable linkage between the personal pathology of John Paul II and the structural pathology of the papal system, then we must conclude that the therapy adopted by the Roman curia to keep the pope on his feet is nothing more than a placebo that must end up causing more harm. Austrian Cardinal Franz König declared in 1995 that "the bureaucratic apparatus of the Vatican has developed its own life to such a level as to take on *(de facto, non de jure)* functions that are proper to collegiality and to consultation with bishops. From that point of view there is still no solution to this problem." The same cardinal had said, just after the sudden death of Pope Luciani in 1978, that "it is necessary to reduce more than has been done up to now, the physical and psychic overload to which the pope is subjected, the burden involved in the office, delegating to others some of the papal functions so as not to exceed the limits of fatigue a human being can tolerate."

Some of these very complex structures go back for centuries and are widely judged today to be no longer appropriate to the needs of the church. Whatever measures can be taken to modify them can only benefit the papacy. In any case, to get rid of procedures that are typical of every worldly and imperial power and of the basic paradigm of absolute sovereignty would seem a solution whose time has come, not only from the viewpoint of analytical verifications but also in order to adapt the Petrine office more fully to the situation of Christianity in the world.

The failure of the strategy of a "new Christendom" has been recognized even by Cardinal Ratzinger. Secularization has developed and spread beyond all anticipation, making it necessary to undertake a profound reevaluation of every Christian form, if Christianity is to survive. A clear awareness of that prospect calls for a serious appraisal of the Christian tradition while it is facing the decisions as to what aspects of the papacy should be retained and what should change.

Ratzinger recognizes that Christian society is being shattered before our eyes by the process of secularization, and he rejects as "false" the view of those who fool themselves by thinking that "faith will again become a mass phenomenon." He notes that "the cultural and public role of the church will no longer be the same as it has presented itself up to now in forms of overlapping relations between church and society," and that "the relationship between church and society continues to change and will presumably evolve in the direction of a non-Christian society."

This, nevertheless, does not cause him to despair. Rather, in the exhaustion of the strategy of a *religio societatis* ("religion of the society") in an era of a quantitatively reduced Christianity, the cardinal prefect of the Congregation of the Doctrine of the Faith under John Paul II continues to entertain the possibility of a more self-aware Christianity. But that prospect forces the church to invest all its energy in developing interior Christians, and in a process of forming consciences, with the object of creating a generation of Christians able to offer new models of life, to present a barrier against universal homogenization and to recover the ability to criticize and oppose the dominant myths and earthly interests.[14]

If the analysis of Ratzinger, in its almost apocalyptic lucidity, is correct, then it follows inescapably that the shape of the papacy on the horizon must reflect the development of the radical crisis of the Christian project to the extent that it survives as a residual form of Constantinian Christendom. This is a papacy that has to redesign itself according to the pattern of the Pastoral Constitution, *Gaudium et spes*, of the Second Vatican Council, notwithstanding the fact that this advance has been too often contradicted by Vatican behaviors and choices: "Since the apostles, their successors and all who help them have been given the task of announcing Christ, Savior of the world, to man, they rely in their apostolate on the power of God, who often shows forth the force of the gospel in the weakness of its witnesses. If anyone wishes to devote himself to the ministry of God's Word, let him use the ways and means proper to the gospel, which differ in many respects from those obtaining in the earthly city."[15] Even when the issue is to undertake the ethico-critical mission in the political order, the document insists that the church must use "all the means and only means proper to the gospel."

The remedy is not indeed in the power of the means but in the awareness of the spiritual purposes of the church. The advice of Saint Bernard of Clairvaux, in *De consideratione* to Pope Eugene III, comes to us from the thirteenth century to illuminate still the papal mission at the end of this millennium: "Authority has been given to you in order that you may share, and not that you may give orders. Yes; act as a servant. Yourself a man, do not try to make other men your servants— you would make yourself the servant of a thousand villainies. Yes, you occupy the first rank, the first rank by excellence; but for what purpose do you occupy it? . . . Even we, therefore, no matter how high an opinion we may have of our prerogatives, let us not hesitate to recognize that a service has been placed on us, not that we have been granted power. . . . And so that you may not think that this has been said solely for humility, and not for truth, here is what the Lord says in the gospel: 'Among pagans it is the kings that lord it over them, and those who have authority over them are given the name of Benefactor.' And he adds: 'This must not happen with you.' Nothing could be clearer: dominion is forbidden to the apostles."[16]

—Translated by Gary MacEoin

Notes

1. *National Catholic Reporter*, Kansas City, MO, vol. 32, # 34 (12 July 1996), pp. 12-14.

2. *Lumen gentium*, 35 and 12.

3. Pierre Vallin, "Le Saint-Siège dans les relations internationales," in *Etudes*, 3853, Sept. 1996, p. 222.

4. Ac 12:5.

5. Vallin, *Etudes*, p. 227.

6. *Rome autrement* (Paris, 1997), p. 105.

7. *Codex iuris canonici*, 362-367.

8. H. J. Pottmeyer, "Lo sviluppo della teologia dell' ufficio papale," in *Chiesa e papato nel mundo contemporaneo*, Giuseppe Alberigo and Andrea Riccardi, eds. (Rome-Bari: Editori Laterza, 1990), p. 18.

9. *La civiltà cattolica*, 3249, 2 November 1985.

10. Mk 8:32.

11. *Das neue Volk Gottes*, Italian translation, *Il nuovo popolo di Dio* (Brescia, 1971).

12. See Klaus Schatz, S.J., "Primato, ministero di comunione," in *Il Regno Attualità*, 8, 1997, pp. 238-245.

13. Lk 22:32.

14. J. Cardinal Ratzinger, *Il sale della terra* (Milan, 1997).

15. *Gaudium et spes*, 76. *Vatican Council II; The Conciliar and Post Conciliar Documents*, Austin Flannery, O.P., ed. (Northport, NY: Costello Publishing Company, 1975), p. 739.

16. Lk 22:25-26.

5

All Religions Are from God

GARY MacEOIN

The acceleration of time and shrinkage of space in the twentieth century made actual for the Catholic church and the papacy a problem that had previously been only theoretical. Thanks to the airplane, the telegraph, the telephone, the television, the Internet, and orbiting satellites, the world has become a single community, admittedly as yet a confused and conflicted community, but none the less a real one.

We had long known—and more concretely since the massive colonization processes begun by Europe in the sixteenth century—that great numbers of human beings existed away out there beyond the limits of culture, limits that were coterminous—at least in our assumptions—with Christendom. Other religions were practiced out there, but they were at best superstitions, at worst inventions of Satan, to be suppressed and, if necessary, exterminated by the sword.

Within this framework, especially as the European expansion revealed obviously superior and indeed irresistible material resources, it was not surprising if we interpreted various texts of scripture as not only committing us to spread the gospel everywhere but as expressing Christ's intention that all human beings should become members of *the one true church*. "Go out to the whole world," he had said. "Proclaim the Good News to all creation. He who believes and is baptized will be saved; he who does not believe will be condemned."[1]

For many centuries this text was taken to mean that no unbaptized person could be saved. Origen, Cyprian, and Augustine were specific: *Extra ecclesiam nulla salus* ("outside the church, no salvation"). Pope Boniface VIII (1294-1303) not only agreed but added a further condition. In the decree *Unam sanctam* he taught that obedience to the pope is a prerequisite for salvation. As with the ark of Noah, he said, so also "outside the one . . . Catholic church there is neither salvation nor remission of sins. . . . Furthermore, we declare, say, define, and proclaim to every creature that they, by necessity for salvation, are entirely subject to the Roman Pontiff."[2] The Council of Florence (1442) added more details:

> The Holy Roman church . . . firmly believes, confesses, and proclaims that outside the Catholic church no one, neither heathen nor Jew nor unbeliever nor schismatic, will have a share in eternal life, but will, rather, be subject to the everlasting fire which has been prepared for the devil and his angels, unless he attaches himself to her [the Catholic church] before his death.[3]

It was possible to think in those terms for as long as cultures were isolated from each other, with the vast majority of people spending their entire lives within a few miles of where they were born. Ignorance allowed the discussion to continue on a high level of abstraction. But a radical change has occurred over the past hundred years. A rapid growth in the total population of the world and a still more rapid growth in our control and utilization of the material resources of the earth forced us to see those "others" as human beings like ourselves. This is how scientist, philosopher, and theologian Teilhard de Chardin, one of the great geniuses of the twentieth century, describes the change.

> Looking back to the turn of the century we see limited wars, clearly marked frontiers, large blank spaces on the map, and distant, exotic lands, to visit which was still like entering another world. Today we have a planet girdled by radio in a fraction of a second and by the aeroplane in a few hours. We see races and cultures jostling one another, and a soaring world population amid which we are all beginning to fight for elbowroom. We see a world, stretched almost to breaking-point between two ideological poles, where it is impossible for the smallest peasant in the

remotest countryside to live without being in some way affected by what is going on in New York or Moscow or China.[4]

In consequence, what happens in one part of the world today affects every other part as never before. The 1988 nuclear accident at Chernobyl will continue to affect the international community for years to come. The depletion of the protective ozone layer in the earth's atmosphere, the pollution of the oceans, and the destruction of much of the Brazilian rain forest—all of these are local events with universal impact.

In this radically changed world, it has become no longer possible for Christians to live with the illusion that their religion, aided by their regular contributions to the work of the foreign missions, was moving rapidly ahead in its worldwide proclamation of the Good News. We had to face the fact that Christianity after twenty centuries was but *one* of the world's great religions. It is true that it had spread so far beyond the European continent which (with its outposts in North America and Australia) had been its historic base, that its center of gravity had shifted to Latin America and Africa. Its gains, nevertheless, were surpassed by those of other religions. Projections for the foreseeable future tell us that its proportion of believers will grow smaller, while other great religions—notably Islam—will increase the proportion of their adherents.

INSIGHTS OF THE SOCIAL SCIENCES

Anthropology has also offered us other insights into the nature of religion. Like language, religion constitutes a major element in every culture. It appears almost everywhere as an integrated element in each culture, giving meaning to real people within a specific historical time frame and cultural context.[5] Every religion, in consequence, has a functional value for its adherents. Or, as Vatican II put it, "other religions which are found throughout the world attempt in their own ways to calm the hearts of men by outlining a program of life covering doctrine, moral precepts, and sacred rites."[6]

Statistics, however, are not the only factor that may reasonably ask us to wonder about the role of religions other than Christianity in the divine dispensation. Many people today are also affected by the problem of justice. Does God show favoritism to some? The question becomes concrete for parents whose child has died without baptism. Why should that innocent child be denied the divine vision that we believe is given to the child that was baptized? More generally, do those who, by accident of birth, are members of the Catholic church have more abundant grace than ninety-nine percent of Chinese or of children born in an aboriginal community in Australia?

Does that mean that religion has become less important or perhaps irrelevant in our radically changed world? Has the movement of secularization inaugurated by the eighteenth-century Enlightenment offered an alternative that is destined to replace religion? The question is valid, but the evidence, both anecdotal and statistical, gives it an overwhelmingly negative answer. Although atheism and agnosticism have become socially acceptable to a far greater extent than ever before in history, the adherents to these alternatives to religion constitute only a very small percentage of the world's population. We now know that the enormous propaganda in favor of atheism in the Soviet Union for several generations had minimal impact on those subjected to it.

For Roman Catholicism the challenge raised today by other religions is traumatic. It can no longer in good faith claim for itself a position of privilege. In the world marketplace of religious ideas, it is but one historic tradition that has to negotiate its place on a level of equality with many others. And by no means is everything in its history likely to impress favorably the non-European cultures to whose members it seeks to appeal.

The growing belief that all religions have a role to play in the divine plan is well expressed by Eugene Hillman, a theologian who has studied African religions for many years.

If this one faith community [Judaism] is seen as an indispensable precondition for the emergence of the divine Word "once-and-for-all" in the physically and culturally tangible terms of human history, then what about all the other pre-Christian faith communities? Are these also, in ways we have hardly begun to think about, preconditions without which the divine Word (incarnated as the sacrament of God) cannot become present through a community of believers (called to be the sacrament of Christ) in the tangible terms of history and culture among all the other particular people who make up and represent symbolically the whole of redeemed humanity? If, moreover, Judaism continues to play a role in the history of salvation after the advent of Jesus Christ, then perhaps the other pre-Christian religions also have a continuing role to play in relation to Christianity.[7]

The reason why this changed interpretation of the religious phenomenon is traumatic for so many Catholics is that once we begin to recognize that religions other than our own have positive values and provide an essential service for their adherents, we can no longer think of them as mere perversions and superstitions, still less the work of Satan. Instead we have to see all religion as a basic human value, a transcendentally grounded and immanently operative system of coordinates, by which we orient ourselves intellectually, emotionally, and existentially. An integral part of the divine plan for humans, religion provides a comprehensive meaning for life, guarantees supreme values and unconditional norms, and creates a spiritual community and home.

What is here involved for Christians is a profound rethinking of our inherited assumptions. Other religions are not enemies to be fought but allies in the attainment of the final purpose of life, which is to bring the created condition to the perfection of which it is capable and which God has wished for it.

AN ENCOUNTER WITH THE HOLY

Hans Küng, who has devoted much study to the meaning and function of religion, insists on its basic role in this process of perfecting the world. Religion, he says, always deals experientially with an encounter with the holy, whether this sacred reality be understood as power, as forces (spirits, demons, or angels), as (a personal) God, as (an impersonal) divine, or as an ultimate reality (nirvana). Religion is a social and individual relationship, vitally realized as a tradition and community (through doctrine, ethos, and generally ritual as well), with something that transcends or encompasses man and his world; with something always to be understood as the ultimate final, the true reality (the Absolute, God, nirvana). In contrast to philosophy, religion is concerned at once with a message of salvation and the way to salvation. It is a lived life, a believing view of life, approach to life, way of life, and therefore a fundamental pattern embracing the individual and society—man and the world—through which a person (though only partially conscious of this) sees and experiences, thinks and feels, acts and suffers, everything. It is a transcendentally grounded and immanently operative system of coordinates, by which we orient ourselves intellectually, emotionally, and existentially. Religion provides a comprehensive meaning for life, guarantees supreme values and unconditional norms, creates a spiritual community and home.[8]

Roman Catholicism has made some tentative steps into this different world, if reluctantly and with at least one step back for every two forward. Its initial reaction in the eighteenth and nineteenth centuries to the Enlightenment, the new philosophy, new science, and new conceptions of the state and of society, of which the American and French revolutions and the Declaration of Human Rights were logical political consequences, was one of horror and rejection. Angered and frightened by the attacks of the revolutionary movements of nineteenth-century Italy which threatened their temporal power, Popes Gregory XVI and Pius IX insisted that the social order was eternally fixed by God and that those "impious men" who sought to change it were driven simply by a hatred of religion.

The important values for humanity of the movement for social change slowly began, nevertheless, to penetrate. The respect for the rights of every individual inherent in democracy could not be resisted forever. The emphasis on historicity made it possible to take a new look at dogma and recognize the difference between objective truth and the historically conditioned forms in which it was expressed. Reflection on the true role of religion made it clear that life was something more than a time of testing for future happiness, that it had its own values worthy of being pursued, that the role of religion was not only to liberate us from sin but also from every situation that prevented the full development of each person's capabilities.

The Catholic church began gradually, in consequence, to expand its awareness that religion has, not only a personal, but also a social role. It does not exist for itself. It exists for the world. It exists for the world, in the first instance, because it offers the world what it does not know, namely, the ultimate truth about God and humans, about salvation and damnation. It exists for the world by being committed to the world, by being involved in the world, by assuming responsibility for the world not only in words but in deeds. To perform these tasks it must join with and support all human structures dedicated to achieving these objectives, and specifically it must engage in dialogue and action with other religions, both Christian and non-Christian, all of which by definition seek the same goals.

INSIGHTS OF THE SECOND VATICAN COUNCIL

The Second Vatican Council (1962-1965) gave legitimacy to many of these currents of thought that had previously existed precariously on the edge of Catholic orthodoxy. The concept of One World acquired a meaning for the first time in the twentieth century, a meaning given concrete expression by the creation of the United Nations in 1945. The geographic horizon of the world, including the religious world, had already changed enormously in recent centuries, thanks to the great European voyages of discovery. So had the historical horizon as the study of world religions developed, a study encouraged by the fact that these religions are no longer separated geographically. Thanks to massive migrations, members of many religions live side by side in practically every country of the world, especially in the big cities. Our neighbors and fellow workers may include Hindus, Buddhists, and Moslems.

In this reading of the Signs of the Times, the Council was enormously helped by Pope John XXIII (1958-1963), whose encyclicals, *Mater et Magistra* and *Pacem in Terris*, opened new horizons. John accepted the actual and objective impulse of contemporary society, which he correctly described as its intense drive to socialization, collectivization, and planetarization, words and concepts obviously inspired by one of the most creative scientists, philosophers, and theologians of the twentieth century, Teilhard de Chardin. John approved, at least by implication, of the ever more complex and interrelated structures of society, as described by Karl Marx, Teilhard, and other social scientists. He insisted that we had acquired a level of control of the material world that should not be left to a few to manipulate for private gain; that such things as nuclear energy, genetic engineering, automation, cybernetics, conquest of space, and instant communications were the inheritance of all so that all should share in their control and benefits.

Thus encouraged by John XXIII, Vatican II set its seal of approval on developments initiated long before within the body of the faithful but continually resisted by the Roman authorities. By the reevaluation of the Bible and preaching, by introducing the vernacular in liturgy, by the active participation of lay people, and by the beginnings of adaptation of church practices to the cultures of various nations, it belatedly accepted major paradigmatic changes introduced to the world of religion by the Protestant Reformation of the sixteenth century. It recognized the human values of modern science, the Copernican world picture, and the long-anathematized Darwinian evolutionary thinking. Also granted the freedom of the city were modern history, modern biblical scholarship, modern democracy, popular sovereignty, freedom of conscience and religion, and human rights as a whole; the new mentality of freedom being institutionalized by the abolition of church censorship and of the Index of Forbidden Books.

Additionally, the Council encouraged radically different ways of thinking about other religions, insisting that it was never God's intention to limit grace to one small segment of humankind. What theologians had been whispering among themselves for a long time, namely, that we Christians could no longer delude ourselves into believing that it was only a question of time until we achieved in fact what has always been our project—to convert all peoples to the one faith—was finally being asserted in public. Given the reality that Christianity is not only a small segment of humankind but a declining proportion of humans, it was essential to find new formulas of coexistence with other religions. This search was all the more urgent because, even within the traditional home of Christianity, increasing numbers were embracing other faiths or abandoning all religious belief and institutional identification.

The Council began its rethinking by stressing what all religions have in common. They offer answers, it said, to the deepest mysteries of the human condition. What is the essence of that condition? What is the meaning and purpose of life? What is goodness and what is sin? What gives rise to sorrow, and why? What is the path to true happiness? What is the truth about death, judgment, and retribution? Why this wondering about an existence beyond the grave, and how legitimate is it?

We are already in a very different world from that of the pre-Vatican II church and, in particular, from that of the church that accompanied the European powers in their conquest of a vast part of the world from the sixteenth to the nineteenth century. Other religions are no longer the inventions of Satan in his unending struggle against God, abominations to be destroyed by fire and sword. Instead, all of them arise from the depths of the human mind in its search for truth.

Thus in Hinduism, said the Council, its devotees

> explore the divine mystery and express it both in the limitless riches of myth and the accurately defined insights of philosophy. They seek release from the trials of the present life by ascetical practices, profound meditation, and recourse to God in confidence and love. Buddhism, in its various forms, testifies to the essential inadequacy of this changing world. It proposes a way of life by which men can, with confidence and trust, attain a state of perfect liberation and reach supreme illumination either through their own efforts or by the aid of divine help. So, too, other religions which are found throughout the world attempt in their own ways to calm the hearts of men by outlining a program of life covering doctrine, moral precepts, and sacred rites.
>
> The Catholic Church rejects nothing of what is true and holy in these religions. She has a high regard for the manner of life and conduct, the precepts and doctrines which, although differing in many ways from her own teaching, nevertheless often reflect a ray of that truth which enlightens all men. Yet she proclaims and is in duty bound to proclaim without fail, Christ who is the way, the truth, and the life (Jn 14:6). In him, in whom God reconciled all things to himself (2 Cor 5:18-19), men find the fullness of their religious life.
>
> The Church, therefore, urges her sons to enter with prudence and charity into discussion and collaboration with members of other religions. Let Christians, while witnessing to their own faith and way of life, acknowledge, preserve, and encourage the spiritual and moral truths found among non-Christians, also their social life and culture.
>
> The Church has also a high regard for the Muslims. They worship God, who is one, living and subsistent, merciful and almighty, the Creator of heaven and earth, who has also spoken to men. They strive to submit themselves without reserve to the hidden decrees of God. . . . [9]

Here we have a relativization of the role of Roman Catholicism, and even of Christianity, in the divine plan that is breathtaking when we recall that the church's highest spokespersons long proclaimed that outside the church there is no salvation.

It may be argued that this and similar statements reflect the inadequacy of language, the need to place everything in its true context. Agreed, but with a corollary. We need to submit our entire Christian language to a more intense examination. How was it created in the course of history? What more or less arbitrary decisions and inferences played a part in each formulation? How definitive are its present expressions?

To start that discussion it may be helpful to see how the church has subsequently dealt with the categorical statements quoted early in this chapter. In the seventeenth century, Rome condemned the similar Jansenist statement: *Extra ecclesiam nulla gratia* ("outside the church there is no grace"). It is not easy to see how one can assert that there is grace outside the church and simultaneously claim that there is no salvation outside it. The Holy Office (now the Congregation for the Doctrine of the Faith) took the matter a step farther in 1952 when it excommunicated Jesuit Leonard Feeney, Catholic chaplain at Harvard University, for asserting along with the old Church Fathers and the Council of Florence that everyone outside the visible Catholic church was damned. And Vatican Council II undertook an even more thorough reversal of "traditional Catholic teaching," when it said: "Men and women who through no fault of their own do not know the gospel of Christ and of his church, but who sincerely search for God and who strive to do his will, as revealed by the dictates of conscience, can win eternal salvation."[10] Actually the so-called traditional teaching that there was no salvation outside the church was not the belief of the first Christians, acquiring popularity only in the fourth century under the influence of Stoic and Manichean notions of human perversity. The earliest tradition based on the concept—formulated in the first chapter of John's gospel—of the Word as "the true light that enlightens all men" stressed God's favor for the "good pagan." Clement of Rome, the third pope (88-97) is quite specific: "From generation to generation the Lord has given opportunity of repentance to all who would turn to him."[11] Justin Martyr (c. 100-165) agrees: "Those who lived by reason are Christians, even though they have been considered atheists: such as, among the Greeks, Socrates, Heraclitus and others like them."[12] Justin Martyr, Clement of Alexandria, and Origen describe Plato, Aristotle, and Plotinus as "pedagogues," guiding their readers to Christ.

Nor did the more rigorous opinion go unchallenged in the Middle Ages. Dante Alighieri (1265-1321), one never to hesitate in consigning friends and enemies to eternal bliss or pain, recorded his view in *Il Paradiso*: "A man is born on the shores of the river Indus, and there is no one to tell him of Christ. . . . All his desires and deeds are good, so far as human reason sees, sinless in life or speech. He dies unbaptized and without faith. Where is that justice that condemns him?"[13] As theologian Eugene Hillman writes

Even the formally promulgated doctrines of the church under the mantle of infallibility are always presented in the garb of particular times and specific cultures. These formulations of belief are more like theological milestones than ultimate terminals of revealed truth. Indeed, it is appropriate to the nature of a pilgrim people that the truth should be understood only in progressive stages.[14]

The Hillman suggestion that we acquire truth in progressive stages seems particularly apposite. In what way, for example, is our idea of God the whole truth? How can we reconcile it with what Vatican II said about Hinduism which is a non-theist religion, with vacuity as the ultimate reality? Nor can we forget that our idea of God is being changed by, for example, the changing role and status of women in our society. It is now possible to refer to God as "she," even if we have not yet drawn all the significance of this change in our ways of thinking. To say that God is woman does not merely get away from the patriarchal image of God as unchallengeable law, the image at the base of religious violence and fanaticism. It helps us to envisage other ways of expressing what we mean by the concept; to make meaningful for us such qualities as compassion that our culture associates with the feminine.

All religions have an eschatological function. They provide a way to salvation, an assurance that a goal exists to strive toward and to which we are all called. As St. Paul put it, "Creation awaits impatiently. . . ."[15] To understand what every religion means, we must focus on the enormous investment of hope and passion it represents, realizing that it exists for a purpose, the ultimate liberation toward which all humans instinctively strive. Just as the insistence that the divine will and the struggle for the Kingdom announced by Jesus are identical is central to Christianity, so is the focus on the future essential to all religions.

The incarnated condition of Christian discourse places it on equal level with the other religious discourses of humanity. If God reveals himself through our tradition, there is no clear frontier cutting this tradition off or apart from neighboring traditions that have often enriched ours. Our religious language is a part of a family of religious languages and part of an immense work of imagination and articulation by which humans seek to express in their many languages the voice of the utterly absolute.

For the first time we are able, in the twenty-first century, to see the world as a whole. Christians can no longer see themselves as the center around which everything else, including all other religions, gravitates. Not only have we access to other cultures by travel and by television, but the other great religions are physically in our midst. In the United States we cannot continue to live with our caricatures of Islam, Hinduism or Buddhism, because there are already enough members of each of these faiths living among us. We know them as individuals, not stereotypes.

Another result of the new world unity is our forced awareness of the fact that, while Christianity has always presented itself as a faith for all humanity, in two thousand years it has not made itself, and as of today it has no prospect of making itself in any remote way, the faith of vast areas of the globe.

Take the case of China, for example. Estimates of the number of Roman Catholics and of other Christians in China vary widely. But the most ambitious estimates do not go beyond one percent. Christianity for the Chinese is not just an irrelevance. It is an enemy, not because Marx or Mao said so, but because the Christianity that China has historically known is the religion that entered with barbarian invaders, counted on them to protect and support it, and legitimized their humiliation of the world's oldest civilization. For the foreseeable future Christianity will make no significant impact on China's one-fifth of the world population.

What practical difference would the kind of rethinking of the role of world religions here proposed make? I am not going to offer arguments about the value of religion. I think I can assume for those who will read this book that they agree that religion is important because it can influence how people live and what they do. What I suggest is that the world religions working together to promote the many objectives on which they agree will achieve their goals far more efficiently and completely than religions that see each other as competitors and, not infrequently, enemies.

Such cooperation would not necessarily exclude missionary efforts by any group. Perhaps it would encourage those who feel a missionary call to concentrate more on the vast numbers of human beings in our splintered world who have no religious knowledge or affiliation. But all it would demand is that all mission approaches respect the beliefs of those addressed and promote their own beliefs in honest but friendly dialogue. The social objective is not to work toward a single world religion. The assumption is that each religion will survive as long as it continues to perform a service for its adherents.

Given all these agreed facts, we have to think quite differently about religions other than Christianity. Far from being the work of the devil, they constitute the result of a high level of human intellectual exploration. Every religion represents a structured response to the questions that each of us must ask and for which we must find an acceptable answer: where have we come from; why are we here; where are we going? Religion is an integral part of the divine plan for humans. It provides a comprehensive meaning for life, guarantees supreme values and unconditional norms, and creates a spiritual community and home.

Since behavior and morality are a specific area of religion, the connection between ecumenism and world peace is obvious. Ecumenical theology can help to discover and work through the conflicts caused by the religions, confessions, and denominations. Before all, it can work to resolve the conflicts for which they themselves are to blame. The cruelest political struggles are those that have been colored, inspired, and legitimized by religion. If we can imagine a world in which all religions see themselves as collaborators in a common project, we are close to a world in which all swords will have been beaten into plowshares.

SPECIAL RELATIONSHIP TO OTHER CHRISTIANS

The obvious and inevitable corollary to this different understanding of our relationship to other world religions is an equally new approach to our relationship as Roman Catholics with other Christian churches and groupings. Here our ultimate objective should be different from our objectives in our relationships with other religions. It should be to bring about corporate reunion: "that all may be one."

There has long been substantial agreement within the major Christian bodies that this is the goal, and significant advance in dialogue has taken place during the past quarter-century. But there is more recently a sense of frustration, a feeling that we are talking past each other.

It seems to me that there are two areas we should try to analyze more thoroughly. One is the order of the steps we must take on the road to union. The other is the form that union should take.

As regards the order, are we perhaps giving too high priority to the legal issues raised by the anathemas and dogmatic statements made by both sides, thinking we can create union from the top down through legalistic reformulations? True union is from the bottom up, from people learning to love each other by living in community.

The Second Vatican Council provided an example of the inadequacy of the legalistic approach. As it closed in December 1965, a joint declaration was published simultaneously in Rome and in Istanbul canceling the mutual excommunications formulated in 1054 when papal legate Cardinal Cerularius deposited the document of excommunication on the altar of Santa Sophia in what was then Constantinople, and the patriarch replied by excommunicating the pope. In legal or canonical terms, the two churches were once again in communion. If you are not excommunicated, you are in communion. But, practically speaking, nothing had changed. The spiritual attitude on both sides has still to be addressed.

This is a point that was well focused by Max Joseph Metzger, a German priest executed by Hitler "for treason" in 1944. In a letter to Pius XII in 1939, Metzger asked the pope to convene a council, arguing that Christians are less divided on doctrine than in "the spiritual attitude on both sides"; that dogmatic differences, though real, are more easily soluble than prejudice born of ignorance.[16] What that means is that union of Christians cannot simply be legislated. A growing together in love is the only way to union.

The other issue we have to face is the form the union must take. Let us start with some pertinent statements from the Second Vatican Council's Decree on Ecumenism:

All those justified by faith through baptism are incorporated into Christ. They therefore have a right to be honored by the title of Christian, and are properly regarded as brothers in the Lord by the sons of the Catholic church. Moreover some, even very many, of the most significant elements or endowments which together go to build up and give life to the church herself can exist outside the visible boundaries of the Catholic church: the written word of God; the life of grace; faith, hope, and charity, along with other interior gifts of the Holy Spirit and visible elements. All of these, which come from Christ and lead back to him, belong by right to the true church of Christ.

The brethren divided from us also carry out many liturgical actions of the Christian religion. In ways that vary according to the condition of each church or community, these liturgical actions most certainly can truly engender a life of grace, and, one must say, can aptly give access to the communion of salvation.[17]

After this very strong expression of the positive values of other Christian bodies, the Council went on to discuss reunion in terms that clearly envisaged a formal reintegration (as the Latin title of the document already suggested: *redintegratio*). Whatever might be said about the desirability of such a form of unity, the likelihood of its occurring is still remote, in spite of the growth of cordial relations among the major Christian churches. It will certainly not happen unless some of the radical changes in the style and pretensions of the papacy proposed in this book by Father Häring and other contributors first come to pass.

The approach of reintegration, it seems to me, is not only unrealistic but unnecessary. The first thousand years of Christianity were marked by the development of a wide divergence in historical forms of orthodox Christianity, in spite of common scriptures and a profession of faith to which most subscribed. There were differences in form and ethos between East and West from very early times. Early medieval Christianity was profoundly changed by the incorporation and subsequent importance of Germanic tribes. Christianity quickly sought accommodation with the total culture of northern Europe. From this came a stratification of laity and clergy, a growing distance between altar and people. Given this long history of adaptation and accommodation, can we not envisage the recognition of the major Christian churches in the West as so many rites, each with its own canonical structures, its mode of government, its charism?

What is definitely possible, and what can be achieved without any of the parties being forced to repudiate their respective theological positions, is an acknowledgment—along the lines set out in the document on ecumenism of the Second Vatican Council—that each is a channel of Christ's grace for its members, and that all of them can and must work together to promote the purposes for which they all exist.

Just how they should coordinate their efforts is a matter to be worked out by mutual agreement. I think that most groups that identify themselves as Christian churches would agree with the Orthodox churches in according a primacy of honor to the bishop of Rome. I am not sure, however, that it would be necessary or appropriate to impose such a condition for church communion. The Vatican Council was emphatic that there is a hierarchy of truths. How high on the list should the definition of papal primacy be? The church got along without it for nearly two thousand years. It hardly seems necessary to set it up as the shibboleth on which to determine membership of the one, holy, Catholic, and apostolic Church of Christ.

The future relations with other religions—both Christian and non-Christian—envisaged here call for a significant change of mentality and of self-understanding for all of us, and in particular for the papacy. We have to understand that law is not the only, or indeed, the primary element in life. The particular legal institutions of the church, as of every society, are to a large extent the result of historical situations and events. The history of the radical changes that have occurred over the centuries in what Catholics believed about salvation outside the church, as briefly described above, has a message for us today. Does it not call us to look for new ways of relating in solidarity with all those inspired by the Creator to worship in ways different from ours?

Notes

1. Mk 16:16.

2. Denzinger, no. 870, *Bulla Unam Sanctam*, 18 November 1302 (Bologna: Edizioni Dehoniane, 1995).

3. Denzinger, no. 1351, *Bulla Unionis Coptorum Aethiopumque, Cantate*

Domino, 4 February 1442, in ibid.

4. Pierre Teilhard de Chardin, *The Future of Man* (New York: Harper and Row, 1964), p. 247.

5. Eugene Hillman, *Many Paths: A Catholic Approach to Religious Pluralism* (Maryknoll, N.Y.: Orbis Books, 1989).

6. *Nostra aetate*, 2, *Vatican Council II; The Conciliar and Post Conciliar Documents*, Austin Flannery, O.P., ed. (Northport, NY: Costello Publishing Company, 1975), p. 739.

7. Hillman, *Many Paths*, p. 53-54.

8. Hans Küng, *Christianity and World Religions* (Maryknoll, N.Y.: Orbis Books, 1993), p. xvii.

9. *Nostra aetate*, 2, 3, *Vatican Council II,* pp. 739-740.

10. *Lumen gentium*, 16, *Vatican Council II,* p. 367.

11. *Epist. 1 ad Cor.*, chap. 7, quoted Hillman, *Many Paths*, p. 28.

12. *First Apology*, chap. 14.

13. *La Divina Commedia, Il Paradiso,* Canto 19, vv. 70-78.

14. Hillman, *Many Paths*, p. 25.

15. Rm 8:19-20.

16. John Hardon, *Christianity in the Twentieth Century* (Garden City, N.Y.: Doubleday, 1971), p. 440.

17. *Unitatis redintegratio*, 3, *Vatican Council II*, pp. 455-456.

6

Superstar or Servant?

ALAIN WOODROW

Throughout the ages, the role of the papacy has developed and grown in magnitude, concentrating ever more power into the hands of one man and his "court" (curia). The sole text in the gospel to use the word *church*, is Matthew 16:18. After his confession of faith at Caesarea Philippi, when Saint Peter professes his belief that Jesus is the Christ, the Son of the living God, he receives the promise "You are Peter, and on this rock I will build my church," together with the keys of heaven and the power of binding and loosing. "The precise interpretation of this passage," says the Oxford Dictionary of the Christian Church succinctly, "on which the claims of the papacy have been based, has been the subject of much controversy."

Many Scripture scholars, and not only Protestant or Orthodox ones, interpret this text as meaning that the primacy of Peter is a primacy of service, not of jurisdiction. And nothing in the New Testament indicates that Peter was to have a successor. We know for certain that Paul arrived in Rome in the year 63 and that shortly afterward Peter followed him there (to be put to death, a year later, under Nero), but there is no documentary proof of the authority exercised by one or other of the apostles in the capital of the Empire.

The early church was a loose federation of episcopal churches. Many bishops were addressed as "pope" *(pappas* in Greek, that is, father). In the East, only the bishop of Alexandria was called "pope," whereas today all Orthodox priests are so addressed, and, in the West, the title is reserved for the bishop of Rome. At the Synod of Pavia, in 998, the archbishop of Milan was rebuked for calling himself "pope," and in 1073 Gregory VII, in a council at Rome, formally prohibited its use by any other bishop than the bishop of Rome. The see of Rome gradually served as a reference in matters of faith, among other apostolic sees, such as Antioch and Alexandria, and Jerusalem before its destruction.

In the second century, Polycarp, bishop of Smyrna, and his disciple Irenaeus, bishop of Lyons, attest to the growing role of the Petrine church as arbiter in matters of doctrine, at least for the Western church. The question, however, is "Whom to believe?"—not "Whom to obey?" Little is known of the first successors of Peter, except that they were elected by the Christian community living in Rome. The era of tolerance ushered in by the Emperor Constantine's conversion in 313 and the recognition by Theodosius, in 391, of Christianity as the official religion of the Empire, led to the subjection of the church to the state.[1] Adopting the political structure of the latter, the Church became "monarchic": the bishops were the "leaders" (on the model of the Roman prefects) of the clergy and, from the fifth century onwards, the pope adopted the title of "Pontifex Maximus" ("supreme pontiff" or "bridge-builder"), originally a pagan title of the chief priest at Rome!

The bishops retained their independence, however; as Cyprian, bishop of Carthage, had stated significantly in 250: "There is no bishop of bishops." When Constantine moved to Byzantium (Constantinople), the pope remained in Rome as "Patriarch of the West." He began to legislate, as the temporal leader of the Imperial capital, publishing his "decretals" which had force of law. The West became "papalist" while the East remained "conciliar." The progressive decline—and fall in 476—of the Roman Empire freed the pope from the emperor's jurisdiction and reinforced his power.

Leo I (440-461) began to expound a theory that would develop in the centuries to come, namely that, as "vicar of Peter," the pope is in charge of the universal Church, which he must govern as the emperors governed the Roman Empire. Gelasius I (492-496) went further, claiming that the "Apostolic See" has a right to judge each local church, while itself subject to no human tribunal. This view was naturally rejected by the Eastern church, for whom the pope is simply "the first among patriarchs." In the eighth century, the French king Pépin le Bref donated land he had won from the Lombards to Pope Stephen I. This was the birth of the Papal States which expanded under successive popes to encompass a large part of Italy and increase the temporal power of the papacy.

The inflation of the papacy led to the extremist views expressed by Gregory VII (1073-1085) and Innocent IV (1243-1254). The struggle between the popes and the Germanic emperors in the twelfth and thirteenth centuries, ending in the victory of the pope over the Holy Roman Emperor Henry IV at Canossa in 1076, encouraged Gregory VII to defend the idea of a theocracy. In his *Dictatus papae* he states: "The Roman pontiff alone can be described as universal; he is the only man whose feet are kissed by all the princes; he has the power to depose emperors." Saint Bernard, who died in 1153, defended the theory of the "two swords" (Lk 23:38). According to him, both swords, spiritual and temporal, belong to the church, but while the former is drawn by the church, the latter is drawn in her defense, and on her command. This theory justifies the Crusades against Islam carried out by Christian princes at the behest of the pope.

The theory, as expounded by Augustine in his *City of God*, is simple. The temporal state only has value insofar as it serves the religious cause for which it was founded. The state is subservient to the church, the sole abiding city, and thus the temporal is contained within the spiritual, and all power within the church. The thirteenth century witnessed the long struggle by the popes—who by then were also the sovereigns of most of Italy—to defend their power against the Empire, and against the young Christian states of France (Philippe le Bel) and England (the Plantagenets), which were fighting for their autonomy. The last pope to invoke the theory of the two swords, Boniface VIII (1294-1303), was vanquished by the French king. Popes who followed him, all French, were obliged to live in Avignon from 1309 to 1377.

The great schism of the West (1378-1417), with as many as three rival popes, weakened the papacy still further and gave birth to the conciliar theory, according to which sovereignty in the church resides in the general councils, to be convoked at regular intervals, and not in the pope alone. The Councils of Constance (1414-1418) and Basel (1431-1448) defined this quite clearly. But once the papacy was reunified after the election of Martin V in 1417, it reclaimed its power over the council, and the Renaissance popes (from Nicholas V to Julius II) even took up arms to defend the Papal States. These popes were worldly princes, humanists, patrons of the arts and often quite immoral.

It was in this context of intrigue and debauch that the great Protestant reformers, beginning with Luther, attacked Rome—"the scarlet woman" and the "whore of Babylon" mentioned in the Apocalypse—and the papacy. To counter Luther's teaching on the universal priesthood of all Christians, the Council of Trent (1545-1563) reaffirmed the masculine, celibate priesthood and set in motion a profound Counter-Reformation, based on the authority of Pius V (1566-1572) and Clement VIII (1592-1605). Destabilized by the religious wars between Catholics and Protestants, by the rise of Jansenism and Gallicanism, and by the advent of the *Aufklärung* ("enlightenment")—which taught the primacy of individual conscience over the teaching authority—a besieged papacy was attacked on all sides.

At the end of the eighteenth century and the beginning of the nineteenth, the tide turned. The humiliation suffered by Pius VI (1775-1799) at the hands of the Directory, in France, and by his successor Pius VII—taken prisoner by Napoleon—led to a movement of sympathy in favor of the pope, which hardened into "ultramontanism" (excessive centralization of authority in the pope and his Curia), thanks to the writings of Félicité de Lamennais and Joseph de Maistre. In postrevolutionary Europe, the papacy appeared the only stable authority and it gradually regained its political credibility. Between 1801 and 1860, eighteen concordats were signed by Pius VII (1800-1823), Gregory XVI (1831-1846) and Pius IX (1846-1878).

The French Revolution was condemned by Pius VI in 1791, and all the popes of the nineteenth century took the same anti-liberal line, up until Leo XIII. The Church condemned in turn the French Revolution, freedom of opinion, the Enlightenment, and all forms of democracy, whether in church or state. Pius IX, who was venerated as "the viceroy of humanity," was the most intransigent pope of the nineteenth century and author of the famous Syllabus of Errors (1864),[2] a catalogue of eighty "principal errors of our time."[3] Its issue was greeted with a storm of protest: in Britain, Gladstone condemned the document, and in France, its publication was forbidden for a time.

CREEPING INFALLIBILITY

This rejection of modern thought and of the world at large imprisoned the church in an "integralist" fortress. To crown the whole edifice, the First Vatican Council (1869-1870) defined the infallibility of the pope, 19 July 1870. The day after the promulgation, war broke out between France and Prussia, and the occupation of Rome by Italian troops brought the Council to an end. Ironically, within two months of being declared infallible, Pius IX finally lost Rome to the *risorgimento* which had succeeded in uniting Italy.

Henceforth, the pope's formidable power would be primarily spiritual and moral. But his every pronouncement would assume a new weight and authority. William Ward, a British theologian—disciple of John Henry Newman and convert to the Roman Catholic Church—who became an extreme neo-ultramontane theological advisor to Cardinal Henry Manning—archbishop of Westminster—claimed that every doctrinal statement of the pope was *ipso facto* infallible. He remarked that he would like nothing better than to find a new infallible statement of the pope every morning at breakfast with his *Times*. "Creeping infallibility" was on the move.

Vatican I is crucial to an understanding of the development of the papacy and the prestige and power of the Vatican in the church today. As Paul Collins writes: "There is a sense in which the papacy of John Paul II is the natural result of all that was decided in 1870."[4] When Pius IX convoked the Twentieth Ecumenical Council (the largest council held until then) on the eve of the Franco-Prussian war, the bishops (more than seven hundred) were divided into two camps: a majority of ultramontanes, in favor of strengthening papal authority and defining papal infallibility, and a liberal minority opposed to the definition, some on tactical, others on theological grounds.[5]

The first group included Archbishops Manning of Westminster and Deschamps of Malines, and Bishops Pie of Poitiers, Martin of Paderborn, and von Senestrey of Ratisbon. Their opinions were relayed by the press, in France by Louis Veuillot in *L'Univers,* and in England by William Ward in *The Tablet* and *The Dublin Review*. In Italy, the powerful Jesuit magazine *La Civiltà Cattolica* espoused the ultramontane view. The liberal minority was represented in the Council by Bishop Dupanloup of Orleans, and most German and many Austrian and American bishops, and—outside the Council—by John Henry Newman in England, and the lay professor of history, Johann von Döllinger in Munich, Bavaria.

The schema *De Romano Pontifice* was criticized by the minority for defining the pope's jurisdiction as "ordinary, immediate, and truly episcopal." With regard to infallibility itself, the minority wanted it to be linked more closely with the infallibility of the church. The definition received 451 *placet* (votes in favor), 88 *non placet* (votes against), and 62 *placet juxta modum* (votes in favor, with reservations). The final constitution *Pastor Aeternus* was passed by 533 *placet* to 2 *non placet*, the remainder of the minority abstaining.

The resulting definition was a compromise that displeased the extremists on both sides. It affirms the pope's infallibility by stating that his definitions are "irreformable of themselves and not from the consent of the Church," but it restricts his infallibility to those occasions "when he speaks *ex cathedra*, that is, when in discharge of the office of pastor and teacher of all Christians, by virtue of his supreme apostolic authority, he defines a doctrine regarding faith or morals to be held by the universal Church."

Unfortunately, the Council did not have time to rectify the imbalance it had created. A schema on the role of the bishops was drafted but it did not see the light of day. As Paul Collins remarks: "This was to have tragic consequences. The pope emerged from the Council in solitary splendor; and with more and more petty centralization of all authority in Rome, the bishops were increasingly seen as mere representatives of head office."[6] Although all the minority bishops rallied to the constitution, it was rejected by some opposition groups in Germany and Austria, who formed the "Old Catholic" church. Döllinger, who refused to submit, was excommunicated, and Austria canceled its concordat with Rome.

After a relative liberalization by Leo XIII (1878-1903)—who laid the basis of papal social teaching in his encyclical *Rerum novarum* (1891), reconciled French Catholics with the Republic, and cautiously encouraged biblical studies and literary criticism of the Scriptures—Pius X turned the clock back by waging war against "Modernism," described as "the mother of all heresies." He not only condemned "65 erroneous propositions" in his decree *Lamentabili*, but unleashed a far-reaching witch hunt against all supposed enemies of the church in his encyclical *Pascendi* (1907), imposing an anti-Modernist oath on all ordinands, bishops, and priests appointed to teaching or administrative posts.

This action had a disastrous impact on Catholic scholarship, and led to the muzzling of some of the finest minds in the church (Alfred Loisy, Friedrich von Hügel, George Tyrrell, then Pierre Teilhard de Chardin, and later, Henri de Lubac and Yves Congar). Convinced that democracy led to a denial of the rights of God, and that the separation of church and state was sacrilegious, Pius X condemned the *Sillon* movement in France, launched by Marc Sangnier, which propagated "democratic Christianity."

Benedict XV (1914-1922) tried to act as mediator between the French and Germans during the First World War by sending his nuncio in Bavaria, Monsignor Pacelli, on a peace mission to the German authorities. He was accused of appeasement by such French intellectuals as Léon Bloy and Father Sertillanges, whereas he was simply ensuring that the Holy See remained neutral. His interest in ecumenism led him to create the Pontifical Oriental Institute in Rome. Above all, he put an end to the worst excesses of the anti-Modernists. His successor, Pius XI (1922-1939), signed the Lateran Treaties in 1929 with Benito Mussolini. The "insoluble Roman question" was finally settled: the Holy See recognized the kingdom of Italy, with Rome as its capital, and the Vatican City became an independent state, receiving substantial financial compensation for the loss of the Papal States.

Faced with the advance of communism, on the one hand, and the rise of Nazism on the other, Pius XI attacked the former in his encyclical *Divini Redemptoris* (1937), and the latter in *Mit brennender Sorge* (1937). He also had to deal with the plight of the church in Mexico and in Spain, principal victim of the civil war. Ruling the church with a hand of iron, the pope increased the authority of the hierarchy, elaborated the complex process for canonizations (he presided over five hundred beatifications and thirty-four canonizations, including the Curé of Ars and Thérèse of Lisieux), and founded the Vatican Radio. He opposed birth control (just after the Lambeth Conference had given a cautious green light to contraception, for Anglicans) and the emancipation of women, but he also created the Catholic Action movement, to encourage the laity to play a more active part in the life of the church.

His secretary of state, Eugenio Pacelli, was elected as Pius XII in 1939, on the eve of the Second World War. His first six years, during the war, remain the subject of controversy concerning his public silence about the Jewish holocaust. Within the church he was far from silent, issuing statements, speeches and encyclicals on every possible topic. In spite of his natural authoritarianism, he modernized the church to a certain extent, admitting the legitimacy of public opinion in the church. In the encyclical *Mystici corporis Christi* (1943), he placed the emphasis on the Christian community rather than the hierarchical church, and in *Divino afflante Spiritu* (1943) he lifted the ban on modern historical and critical methods in scriptural exegesis. But his encyclical *Humani generis* (1950)—directed against the "new theology" in France, and especially the writings of the Jesuit paleontologist Teilhard de Chardin—put the brake on creative thinking. Politically more anti-communist than anti-fascist, he condemned communism as "intrinsically perverse," whereas he signed a concordat in 1953 with Franco's fascist regime.

The election of John XXIII in 1958 marked a watershed in the history of the papacy in this century. His inspired decision to convene the Second Vatican Council (1962-1965), against the advice of "the prophets of doom," unleashed a refreshing wind of change and opened the Church's windows onto the contemporary world. Fundamentally optimistic, "good Pope John" stated that the Council was not about condemning errors—"We prefer the medicine of mercy to severity"—but intended to realize the *aggiornamento* ("updating") of the church and reunification with "our separated brethren."

The largest Council in the church's history, the 2,640 voting participants were soon divided into an open-minded majority, led by the French bishops, notably Cardinal Achille Liénart of Lille, and their *periti* (theological experts Yves Congar, M.-D. Chenu and J. Daniélou), Cardinal J. Frings of Cologne (with his advisor the Swiss theologian Hans Küng), Cardinal Bernard Jan Alfrink of Utrecht (with his advisor Edward Schillebeeckx), and Cardinal de Smedt of Bruges; and a conservative minority, under the banner of Cardinal Alfredo Ottaviani (prefect of the Holy Office) and Archbishop Marcel Lefebvre (formerly of Dakar, Senegal, later excommunicated as schismatic).

The major gains of the Council include a new positive approach to non-Catholic Christians, to non-Christians, and to non-believers; the decentralization of the church through a vernacular liturgy and a limited "inculturation"[7]; and the recognition of episcopal and local synods, episcopal conferences, and ecumenical bodies. But the greatest task was the attempt to restore the balance between the pope and the rest of the church. The first victory was won in overturning the schema of the church by putting the laity ("the people of God") before the hierarchy. The third chapter, on the collegiality of the bishops, was vital in counteracting the excessive power given to the pope by Vatican I's definition of his infallibility and primacy. The conservative minority scored a point in their favor when they succeeded in introducing an "explanatory note" into the chapter on collegiality (with the consent of Paul VI, elected in 1963) excluding any encroachment by the college of bishops on papal primacy.

In spite of his intelligence and broadly progressive frame of mind—he was greatly influenced by the new French theology—Paul VI remained a tortured, timid man, torn "Hamlet-like" between tradition and reform. His prime objective was to secure the unity of the church by engineering a consensus, or at least moral unanimity, for the Council's decisions. As a result, he vacillated, removed certain controversial subjects from the Council's agenda (such as clerical celibacy), and finally weakened the reforming thrust of the Council by giving in to the hardliners (two or three hundred reactionary bishops had formed a resistance group, closed to all change).

He certainly saved the church from open schism (apart from the small Lefebvrist group); but at the cost of decisive leadership and a failure to give the church a clear blueprint for the future. His greatest failure was on the issue of collegiality. He ignored the majority opinion of the commission he had set up to examine the ruling on birth control, reaffirming the ban in his encyclical *Humanae vitae* (1968). Above all, he finally refused to give the synod of bishops any real decisional power, such as, for example, the election of the pope, preferring what he called "affective" collegiality to an authentic episcopal force that might threaten papal prerogative. Vatican I remained the norm regarding the primacy of the pope, as John Paul II was soon to prove.

THE SINGER, NOT THE SONG

After the brief interlude of John Paul I, the election of the Polish Cardinal of Cracow as John Paul II, in 1978, brought the conciliar era to an abrupt end. The first non-Italian pope since 1522, the charismatic and vigorous Karol Wojtyla—in spite of his continual lip service to the Council—has achieved a general "restoration" in the Catholic Church. By multiplying the number of papal nuncios and other representatives of the Holy See to international organizations; nominating numerous conservative bishops, often against the express wishes of the local churches; and preaching an intransigent doctrine, especially concerning sexual ethics (birth control, abortion, extra-marital relations, divorce, clerical celibacy, and so on), John Paul II has been constantly at the center of attention, replacing or drowning out all other voices in the church. His countless "pastoral" voyages around the world have turned him into a media "superstar."

Whereas Paul VI was modest, hesitant, and unwilling to carry through his reforms to their logical conclusion, John Paul is self-assured, convinced of his "divine mission," and determined to drag the church—kicking and screaming if need be—into his own vision of the twenty-first century, a vision shaped by his Polish ecclesiology and sustained by his theological certainties. No soul-searching or admission of doubt here, but a ringing war cry: "Be not afraid!" I am the pope and I know best!

Paul VI reformed the Curia, but increased its staff from 1,322 in 1960, to 3,146 in 1978, he limited the age of the pope's electors to 80, and asked bishops to tender their resignation at 75, but decided not to apply this ruling to the papal office (although he toyed with the idea); and he refused the suggestion that the universal synod of bishops should replace the college of cardinals as papal electors. John Paul II, on the other hand, considers that the Council, with its freedom of discussion and openness to the modern world, is a closed chapter. He is "for the Council" certainly, but a Council seen as a point of arrival not a point of departure for the future development of the church. He firmly closed the windows so optimistically thrown open by John XXIII, and decided that the church must recover its "identity," become "visible" once again, and re-evangelize a de-Christianized Europe.

The authority of the pope, as defined by Vatican I and scarcely tempered by Vatican II's Dogmatic Constitution on the Church, is intact. This theological vision of the pope as an absolute monarch is not only contrary to the gospel, it is impossible to put into practice. Contrary to the gospel, because it leads to an excessively centralized, bureaucratic church, which tries to control every aspect of Christian life from a narrow European, and even Roman, point of view. Born in the Middle East, the gospel is increasingly imprisoned in the narrow confines of a Western, Latin vision of the world (deprived of the oriental contribution to Christianity since the schism between East and West in 1054) and the juridical strait-jacket of Roman Canon Law.

Impossible to put into practice, because a single man cannot run a worldwide church of 976 million people and, as in all autocratic, non-democratic institutions, the pope's administration (the Curia) is tempted to speak in his name—often without his knowledge. Thus the fiction of "papal documents" (usually drawn up by committees), "papal condemnations" (often instigated by the Congregation for the Doctrine of the Faith, which accuses theologians without "due process"), and other "papal" decisions. The older a pope gets (and he is elected for life), the less he can personally oversee the running of the church.

The exercise of the papal office depends largely on the personality of the incumbent. John Paul II is a strong, authoritarian pope who leaves no doubt as to who is boss. He is the sole master on board, under God, and as he claims to be alone capable of interpreting God's will, there is little room for a "loyal opposition" in the church! Paradoxically, this globetrotting pope is both omnipresent, at the helm of the church, and yet too often absent from Rome. Two jokes heard in Rome express this: "The pope really should add to his full agenda of pastoral visits a short halt at the Vatican," say those who feel that the central government of the church is a full-time job; while others describe John Paul II as "a full-time Pole and a part-time pope," referring to the influence of the pope's Polish entourage, especially his personal secretary, Stanislaw Dziwisz.

John Paul II has a very personal style of government. He consults widely but decides alone, and often in contradiction to the advice received. In Spain, for example, he ignored the criticism by the episcopal conference of the controversial movement *Opus Dei* ("the work of God") and proceeded to change its status from secular institute to personal prelature. In Italy, he encouraged the politically right-wing movement *Communione e Liberazione*, in spite of the warning delivered by the Italian hierarchy. In France, he denounced the new catechetical methods adopted with the bishops' approval. And, as we have seen, the synod of world bishops held regularly in Rome has become a mere rubber stamp of the pope's views. The bishops have even abandoned their consultative role: instead of drawing up a final document, they hand in their conclusions to the pope, who subsequently issues an "apostolic exhortation" bearing little resemblance to the synod debate. When the pope has decided something, he expects to be obeyed without question. Whether it be clerical celibacy, the ordination of women, religious dress, or priests in politics, his word is law and no discussion is tolerated. The qualities he admires, such as obedience, discipline, Marian piety, and powerful ecclesiastical institutions capable of standing up to the secular state, are obviously the ones he knew in his native Poland, qualities he also finds in the "muscular Christianity" practiced by *Opus Dei, Communione e Liberazione*, the *Focolari*, and the neo-catechetical movement.

He has difficulty in understanding—or at least in accepting—the anti-triumphalist, democratic, pluralist, and tolerant approach, redis-covered by the Council and much closer to the teaching of Jesus of Nazareth, who came to serve, not to be served. Instead of the *église servante et pauvre* ("poor and servant church," a phrase coined by Yves Congar), the pope seems to have opted for the Polish model of a powerful and dominant church. He cannot understand why, in Italy for example, the forty million Catholics do not use their numerical force to defend the church's teaching on divorce and abortion. Individual conscience, pluralism of ideas, and respect for the secular state are foreign to his *Weltanschauung.*

The old tag, *Roma locuta, causa finita est* ("Rome has spoken, the dispute is ended"), still holds sway in the Curia but is no longer opera-tive in the church. In spite of its inconclusive character, the Council did promote a certain number of ideas—such as the pre-eminence of the conscience, religious freedom, and the truth found in non-Catho-lic and non-Christian religions—that have steadily undermined the pre-conciliar fortress erected by the Council of Trent. For many Catholics, especially those born since Vatican II, there is no going back. This explains why John Paul II's doctrinal message is rejected by so many. If "the faithful" still turn out in vast numbers to cheer the pope on his travels, it is to applaud the charismatic figure—the hero who helped to demolish the Iron Curtain and braved the assassin's bullet—not his retrograde message. The crowds admire the singer, not the song.

The limited decentralization achieved by the Council, not to speak of the sheer size of the Catholic church, renders impossible a unique message for all. The pope's speeches on his pastoral visits are often a compromise between Roman principles and local situations. Although the local hierarchies remain silent when they receive the pope, they have contributed to the drafting of his speeches, and that explains the difference of tone adopted by the pope in different countries. Indi-viduals sometimes speak out courageously to challenge the papal mes-sage,[8] and some bishops are braver than others. The American hierar-chy published a statement on nuclear disarmament that is much more radical than the position of the Holy See. And on the very day that the pope issued a declaration in Rome forbidding the political involve-ment of priests, Cardinal Basil Hume, archbishop of Westminster, speaking at the national conference of priests in Birmingham, urged them to "play a more active part in the life of the nation, such as trade unions, local government, and parliament."

Religious orders, often more independent of Rome than the secular clergy, and imbued with the conciliar spirit, have been at the forefront of reform. The most striking example is that of the Society of Jesus, which voted in favor of "a preferential option for the poor" and placed "the service of faith and promotion of justice" at the heart of its reform. Irritated by the avant-garde positions of their former General, Pedro Arrupe, especially in Latin America, the pope finally intervened, replacing the ailing Arrupe by two "personal delegates" and ordering "the light cavalry of the Church to dismount," in the colorful phrase of Arrupe's assistant delegate, Fr. Pittau.

Although John Paul II forbids his clergy to engage in politics (i.e., *left-wing* politics) he himself does not hesitate to enter the fray. His constant voyages around the world have been criticized for their cost (usually borne by the country receiving him, including non-Catholic tax-payers); for their highly mediatized, triumphalist trappings (open-air rallies, the parading of the pope in a bullet-proof Popemobile, excessive TV coverage); and for their one-man-shows (the pope, omnipresent, is the only one to speak, to warn, to admonish, rarely to learn and listen), but their ambiguity is primarily political. If the pope stresses the "pastoral character" of these visits, intended to "confirm the faith of his brethren," he cannot avoid their political character.

In 1981, for example, his visit to the Philippines was overshadowed by the presence, at every step, of the dictatorial couple Ferdinand and Imelda Marcos, who profited from this papal acceptance. His visit to Great Britain and then to Argentina during the Falklands war was even more controversial. Whereas the British made sure that the pope met no politicians, the Argentines capitalized on the visit. The pope met military dictator General Leopoldo Galtieri on three occasions, one in the presence of the whole junta. Aware of the trap, John Paul II admitted that he accepted the risk of being branded a "political pope." After the loss of the Papal States, Pius IX declared himself to be "a prisoner of the Vatican," which he never left until his death, and his three successors followed his example. Paul VI was the first modern pope to undertake international voyages, but far from the scale of John Paul II.

In visiting the world's trouble spots (Argentina, Ireland, Lebanon, Bosnia) he has returned to the practice of the medieval temporal popes—makers and deposers of princes. He agreed to act as mediator in the quarrel between Argentina and Chile over the Beagle Canal, and recently the Portuguese president asked his help in solving the crisis in East Timor, illegally occupied by Indonesia. The political status of the pope, both head of state and head of the church, is ambiguous. His interventions are often one-sided, motivated by his personal convictions. Are some dictators better than others? Human rights are indivisible and many criticized the pope for not attending the funeral of Oscar Romero, archbishop of San Salvador, assassinated by the rightwing military dictatorship as he was celebrating mass.

Last but not least, the present inflated role of the papacy in Roman Catholic ecclesiology is a serious stumbling block to Christian unity. The image of the pope as supreme authority in matters of doctrine and discipline—a media "superstar" who occupies all functions and settles all disputes, religious or secular, private or political—is hardly one to reassure Orthodox and Protestant Christians who have rejected an all-powerful papacy and a highly centralized church. Many of them are ready to reconsider their position and some are even willing to accept the spiritual role of the bishop of Rome as a symbol of unity, insofar as he occupies the apostolic see of Saint Peter, but certainly not as the absolute and infallible monarch at the head of a disciplined army.

It is obvious that the first task of the next pope will be to redefine his pontifical office. Of course one could dream of the abolishment of the Vatican as an independent State, the disbandment of the Curia as anachronistic and unnecessary, and the transfer of the papal residence from St. Peter's Basilica to Saint John Lateran, the diocesan church of Rome.[9] Just as the papacy finally profited from the loss of the Papal States, so it would gain in stature and freedom by giving up the fiction of statehood. As spiritual head of the church, the pope would gain credibility, just as the Dalai Lama has achieved a worldwide influence as a "spiritual exile," far greater than what he enjoyed as the temporal ruler of Tibet. If collegiality were to function properly, there would be no need for papal nuncios; and if the synod of bishops were accorded its full legislative role, the college of cardinals would become obsolete.

More realistically, I would argue for a return to the practice of the early church where the pope was accepted by his brother bishops as *primus inter pares* ("first among equals"), because he occupied the primatial see. As bishop of Rome, he was a role model and final arbiter in doctrinal disputes. As "servant of the servants of God," he fulfilled a humble service rather than a magisterial role. The church is not a worldwide multinational organization with the pope as its director, but a communion of individual churches, each governed by its bishop, successor of the apostles: *ubi episcopus, ibi Ecclesia* ("where the bishop is, there is the church"). The pope is first and foremost the center of unity of the church. To be Catholic (as an individual, a bishop or a church) one must be in communion with the bishop of Rome.

The solution to the problem would be to overturn this top-heavy, hierarchical pyramid—something the last Vatican Council began to do in defining the Church as "the people of God." There are several means to this end: firstly, implementing the principle of subsidiarity (a higher authority should never accomplish what a lower echelon is capable of); secondly, accepting more democracy in the church (the local election of bishops by priests and faithful, and legislative authority given to local and general synods; a greater role for the laity in the parish; the accession of women to all ministries; and so on); thirdly, promoting the inculturation of the Gospel (allowing local liturgical rites, the development of non-Roman theologies, respect for the diversity of cultural traditions, etc). And fourthly, accepting a greater delegation of authority (allowing the laity, deacons, and catechists to hold services and administer the sacraments in the absence of priests; and entrusting more pastoral work to the religious—especially nuns).

I would suggest that the next pope immediately convoke a special synod of the principal archbishops of the world to examine two priorities: to define the respective roles and authority of pope-and-Curia and pope-and-synod, and to rescind the canon on the nomination of bishops by the pope.

The papacy is a human institution that has undergone many historical vicissitudes. It is time for a new metamorphosis. After the pagan "pontifex maximus," the Renaissance "worldly prince," and the modern "director of a multinational corporation," why not return to the gospel's job description? "A dispute also arose between them about which should be reckoned the greatest, but he said to them: 'Among pagans it is the kings who lord it over them, and those who have authority over them are given the title of Benefactor. This must not happen with you. No; the greatest among you must behave as if he were the youngest, the leader as if he were the one who serves. For who is the greater: the one at table or the one who serves? The one at table surely? Yet here am I among you as one who serves.' "[10]

Notes

1. Constantine described himself as "bishop of the exterior" and, as such, convoked and presided over the Council of Nicaea (325).

2. The Syllabus was actually drawn up by a Barnabite priest, Luigi Bilio, but it represented the pope's view, all eighty theses having been condemned by him in earlier pronouncements.

3. The ten headings dealt with the following subjects: 1. Pantheism, naturalism, and absolute rationalism; 2. Moderate rationalism; 3. Indifferentism and latitudinarianism; 4. Socialism, communism, secret societies, Bible societies, and liberal-clerical societies; 5. The Church and its rights; 6. Civil society and its relation to the church; 7. Natural and Christian ethics; 8. Christian marriage; 9. The temporal power of the pope; and 10. Modern liberalism.

4. Paul Collins, *Papal Power* (London: HarperCollins, 1997).

5. Those who considered it inopportune to define papal infallibility included Cardinals von Schwarzenberg (Prague), Rauscher (Vienna), and Guidi (Bologna); all the Hungarian bishops; Archbishop Kenrick (St. Louis); and bishops Dupanloup (Orleans), Moriarty (Kerry) and Strossmayer (Bosnia). Those who had theological objections included French Gallicans like Bishop Maret, professor of theology at the Sorbonne, and Hefele (Rottenbury), an eminent historian, and author of a nine-volume history of the councils.

6. Collins, *Papal Power*, p. 56.

7. The introduction of the gospel message into a given culture while respecting local traditions.

8. Sister Teresa Kane, for instance, addressed the pope in the United States to plead for the opening to women of all ministries in the church.

9. In 1950, Cardinal Montini (the future Paul VI) declared: "One day, a pope will divest himself of the cloak of temporal power. He will leave the Vatican and its salaried employees for St. John Lateran, where he will live among his seminarians and his people."

10. Lk 22:24-27.

7

Jubilee 2000 and the Quality of Life

FRANCIS X. MURPHY, C.Ss.R.

In preparation for a cosmic celebration of the Third Millennium, Pope John Paul II has issued an invitation to leaders of the world's religions, as well as members of his own flock, to prepare for what can only be termed a mystagogic prayer experience hopefully to be terminated on Mount Sinai near Jerusalem. In his Apostolic Letter *Tertio Millenio Adveniente* ("on the approach of the third millennium") the Polish pontiff has outlined a series of prayers, liturgical celebrations, theological meditations, and ecclesial functions based on a Trinitarian unfolding of the presence of the Father, the Word and the Holy Spirit in the modern world. In so doing, the pope has suggested the need for a better understanding of the signs of hope present in the last part of this century, even though they often remain hidden from our eyes.

In society in general, the pontiff asserts, such signs of hope include: scientific, technological, and especially medical progress in the service of human life; a greater awareness of our responsibility for the environment; efforts to restore peace and justice where they have been violated; and a desire for reconciliation and solidarity among different peoples, particularly in the complex relationship between the North and the South of the world (par. 46).

Some forty years earlier, almost in anticipation of this optimistic appraisal of the church's attitude toward earthly things, Archbishop Denis Hurley of Durban delivered a discourse to a medical association in India in which he described the church's ambiguous attitude toward

90

the "Quality of Life" down the ages. As a primary consideration, the phrase evoked the image of finding the time and space for nature, art, friendship, and religion. At the same time, it evoked the image of a crushed and crowded subhuman existence lacking all the better things of life.

Actually the church's concern with the quality of life is only a century or so in appreciable existence. While engaged down the centuries in the pursuit of learning, art, and holiness, it seemed unable to enunciate its involvement with the quality of life, due to an ambivalence that dogged Christianity from the beginning. It was an ambivalence about the world and earthly things that early began to infect Christianity.

To what extent this ambivalence was present in the Judaism into which Christ was born is difficult to say. Earlier Judaism battled unflinchingly to reject it. It was the infection of Mesopotamian dualism. In the Mesopotamian cultures, a religion flourished which ascribed the creation of the world to a good God as well as an evil influence. Since evil was so prevalent and so difficult a phenomenon to explain, it was reasonable enough to conclude that with so much evil around, an evil deity must have been responsible; and that it had managed to infect the world and humankind with a terrible malignity.

Judaism had reacted vigorously against this idea. The first book of the Jewish scriptures hammers out the truth that there is only one God, that he created all things, and in regard to everything he created, "he saw that it was good." Indeed after finishing the job with the creation of mankind, "God saw all he had made, and indeed it was very good" (Gn 1:31).

While there was no dualism here, the Mesopotamian dualism lived on and came into contact with the early Christian belief in the form of gnosticism. Anchored on the Greek word for knowledge—*gnosis*—it assured the adept that through knowledge of his inner self, he recognizes the divine origin of his inner being and thus the cause of his enslavement in the flesh, the source of his embodiment. As propagated by the third-century prophet Mani, gnosticism in the form of Manicheism quickly established itself in North Africa, involving, originally, even so brilliant a mind as that of St. Augustine. While eventually returning to the true faith, Augustine seems never to have quite freed himself of its basic influence, thus harnessing the church in the West with a pessimistic attitude toward sin, guilt, and the need for repentance. Its influence seems present in the extreme forms of asceticism indulged by some early Christians and their problem in accepting marriage and the bodily union of man and woman as compatible with Christian standards.

Living as they were—in a world of power and cruelty, of ambition, ostentation, and sexual obsession—one can understand how in their religious fervor many early Christians saw little but evil in the world and in the flesh.

The Jews of earlier times had no such problems in this regard. The Psalms indicate how they revelled in creation, and their frequent use of marriage as a symbol of God's love for his people is a sign of their healthy acceptance of what God had seen in Genesis to be very good. There is, however, a question as to whether the primitive Christians were in some way affected by a dualism that seems traceable, for example, in St. Paul's frequent reference to the "flesh" for what is evil and deviant in man.

In like fashion, when it became necessary to confront the cultural world, the earliest Christian philosophers turned to Plato, one of whose primary concerns was the spirituality of the soul. Unfortunately, Plato in his enthusiasm for the spiritual soul went too far. He had minimized the physical. He had come to see man as spirit imprisoned in the flesh. His view, as accepted by Christian thinkers, confirmed the dualism that was creeping in from other sources.

Throughout its history the church battled strenuously to oppose formal doctrines that tended to regenerate or revive dualism in some form of Manicheism. Consider the ferocity with which it attacked the Catharists of Albi in France in the thirteenth century. Thus an attitudinal ambiguity persisted in regard to the world and the flesh. It was fostered by the popularity of the monastic life which held up monks and nuns with vows as models of authentic Christianity, with a tendency to force clerical life into the same patterns. No doubt in the early Dark Ages and the Middle Ages, community life was the best safeguard for celibacy and prayer. But with priests, monks, and nuns making up the first category of Christians, the laity with no theology of their state, or of marriage or of secular involvement, were quickly reduced to second-class citizens. They were granted their right to marry, to make money, and to settle secular disputes. In the liturgy, likewise, there was a reflection of this clerical attitude that saw mankind as "poor banished children of Eve, weeping and wailing in this vale of tears."

At the same time, the church was praying that we "might despise earthly things and find joy in partaking of the gifts of heaven."

Meanwhile, almost unaffected by this pessimistic strain, the western monastic movement with Benedict of Nursia's *Ora et Labora* ("pray and work") had discovered a formula that eventually produced the dynamic Christendom of the Middle Ages, and in turn led up to the explosion that produced the Renaissance. With the wars of religion that followed the Reformation, and the powerful effects of the Enlightenment, a wholly new style of thinking, and of life, confronted the church of the twentieth century.

While medieval and Renaissance popes had countenanced anti-Semitism, Pope John XXIII—in his first significant actions as Supreme Pastor—had halted the pascal liturgy to eliminate the traditional prayer for "the perfidious Jews." He also created the Vatican Secretariat for Christian Unity, headed by Cardinal Augustin Bea, to deal with Vatican-Jewish relations. John was apparently affected by his experience as papal delegate in Turkey and Greece during World War II in which he had aided numerous Jews to escape Nazi persecution. His successor Paul VI, visited Jerusalem where he met the Orthodox patriarch of Constantinople, Athenagoras, before promulgating the Council decree *Nostra aetate* exculpating the Jews from the charge of deicide. He then set out on a series of jet-hopping visitations beginning with the United Nations in New York and then on to all five continents, thus carrying out Christ's command to preach his gospel to every nation.

His successor, John Paul II, besides having been brought up in close daily contact with Jewish neighbors and school fellows, visited Rome's ancient Jewish synagogue and established diplomatic relations with the Jewish State of Israel. His theology reflects a deep involvement with the Old as well as the New Testament.

Meanwhile the Polish pontiff had literally visited the whole world in some ninety major overseas visitations of countries and cities, many of them grave danger zones where the pontiff fearlessly preached peace and reconciliation as well as justice and the forgiveness of international debts for impoverished nations, while invariably condemning the use of contraceptives.

There is a mystery behind John Paul's challenge to the secular wisdom in the matter of artificial contraception. As a university professor and counselor to young couples he had written a book, *Love and Re-*

94   FRANCIS X. MURPHY, C.Ss.R.

sponsibility, that was extremely explicit in discussing marital relations. Written to care for the problems of an elite group, it sustained the traditional ban on birth control. Wojtyla was a member of the episcopal commission on family life, but he did not attend any of the final meetings. He knew very well, nevertheless, that it was a maneuver by Cardinal Alfredo Ottaviani that intimidated Paul VI into retaining the church's ban.

Despite the fact that well over half the Catholic church's young married couples practice some type of contraception—while the majority of confessors and theologians are silent about the ban—the Vatican and Pope John Paul II continue, even strenuously, to condemn what the pope has labeled a "culture of death." Actually with the tremendous propaganda being exercised by philanthropic, scientific, and both governmental and private organizations, from clinics to health departments and medical experimental organizations all over the world, the papal stand is of a voice of one crying in the wilderness.

What is so excruciatingly enigmatic in this instance is the fact that the current pontiff is an exceedingly intelligent individual with unprecedented worldwide experience who not only banters with the media representatives on his jet-set excursions, but invites outstanding visitors—scientists, sociologists, bankers, doctors, teachers and politicians—to overnight colloquia at Castel Gandolfo regarding world affairs. In addition, he consults regularly with the world's bishops and spiritual leaders.

While still intent on holding the line on such issues as abortion, sterilization, and birth control, the Vatican has seen the necessity of accepting with specific demurrers the general resolutions of United Nations convocations, such as the recent meeting on world health at Cairo and the Beijing convocation on women's rights. In a radical change of direction, the Vatican delegation at Beijing was headed by a woman, a Harvard law professor.

Despite vigorous papal condemnations of secularism synthesized by Pope Pius IX's 1864 Syllabus of Errors, Leo XIII's 1891 encyclical, *Rerum novarum,* finally recognized that, with the rise of secularism, a whole new civilization—scientific and technical—was growing up and growing away from the church.

New values had begun to emerge such as the supremacy of human reason and the sacredness of human freedom. Amid the fierce political tensions of the age, people were beginning to suspect that God was yielding his place to man as the center of gravity.

Instinctively, the church began to feel that the long-overlooked laity were the key to the situation. In a century or so, the world of clerical and monastic priorities had been turned upside down. Now the much despised secularism was gaining the upper hand. And it was only the laity that was capable of confronting this new phenomenon with the skills and competence required by a new type of professionalism.

Likewise, the social situation caused by the Industrial Revolution, which socialist and communist leaders were busily exploiting, could only be handled by a well-educated laity. Thus Catholic Action was inaugurated, giving the laity an involvement in the church's secular as well as religious affairs.

Side by side with these movements, a new interest began to arise in the liturgy and catechetics, and in bible studies and theology.

By a not so strange coincidence, these movements began to center on the laity who by baptism are members of the Body of Christ and share in Christ's role as priest, prophet, and subjects of the Kingdom. Lay people of course do many things beyond fulfilling their spiritual obligations. They buy and sell; they marry and beget children; and they work and promote art, industry, science, law, and medicine, and the whole gamut of culture. They do not do these things to while away the time until they are called into eternity. Neither are they "poor children of Eve, weeping and wailing in a vale of tears" while there are so many wonderful things to do.

Somehow, in the wake of dualism, a negative attitude had prevailed in Christian thinking for 1,900 years and it was inadequate to the Christian appreciation of a divine presence in the world. It was at this juncture in the church's self-evaluation inaugurated by Pope John XXIII, with the publication in the late 1950's of Teilhard de Chardin's *The Divine Milieu* and his *The Phenomenon of Man*, that the basis of a new creational theology was provided for the Council.

All of a sudden, the gray mental baggage that had been the church's inheritance by devious ways from Mesopotamia and the school of Plato through the vale-of-tears theology melted in the glare of Teilhard's genius. Creation rose up again as the work of God. The first chapter of Genesis took on new meaning and Teilhard's favorite passages in St.

John and St. Paul (Jn 1:1-3 and Col 1:15-17) revealed the glorious vision of the cosmic Christ—Jesus not only responsible for the mystery of redemption but also, as the Word of the eternal Father and co-giver of the Spirit, the incarnate Agent of ongoing creation.

Teilhard's two passions—his appreciation of the significance of matter as the substance of creation and his concern with the divinity of Christ—had led him to an acceptance of the theory of evolution, not of course as the result of sheer chance, but as a phenomenon that was going somewhere guided by a divine force. It provided a progression from the unstructured, the manifold, and the material to an ever-growing organization, complexification, and spiritualization. When it began, as exemplified by the Big Bang hypothesis, it was a shapeless mass of atomic particles. Currently it is a mighty pyramid of achievements by a noosphere whose proportions are hard to fathom considering the immense magnitude of the expanding universe.

At the same time there seems to be a fatal flaw that mars our magnificent capacities—the fact that we cannot stand each other, that animosity and conflict are of our very nature. And yet there is in all human beings the capacity to rise above our own aggressiveness; the capacity to match our ability for intellectual reflection; the capacity for personalization, for becoming more and more ourselves by becoming more open to others—all others; and the capacity for love, universal love. Human creativity, human reason will succeed only if guaranteed by human love.

It is here that Teilhard makes his supreme postulate. If evolution has happened, and if it has culminated in hominization, and if hominization implies both socialization and personalization, and if a necessary endowment of both is love, and love is the indispensable condition for all further evolution, there must be an ultimate magnet and drawing force for this converging avalanche of human effort and human affectivity that requires an overpowering personal love ultimately responsible for all other love.

In his capacity as a scientist, Teilhard postulates the existence of such a force, though he does not name it but designates its existence as the Omega Point. Then as a Christian reaction, his faith has him turn the page and proclaim that the Omega Point is Christ.

In this light, creation is a sacred happening and evolution is ongoing creation activated by God through his Incarnate Word. After those long years of vale-of-tears existence, we can finally turn to the Psalms of the Old Testament and rejoice and exult in God's work of creation and take our part in it as God's co-creators. After the long years of estrangement, the mystery of creation has been reconciled with the mystery of redemption. A fusion is taking place that, for religion and culture, has the potential of a hydrogen bomb. For if Christianity can be so dynamic as an aspiration while still suspicious of creation, what will it be when it embraces it? Despite Teilhard's difficulties with the official church, his ideas burst on the world and the church just in time to be a major influence on Pope John's Vatican Council (1962-1965).

The Council was a kind of atomic fusion, too, bringing together all those waves of reform that had been gathering momentum from the beginning of the twentieth century. The world of the Council was a very different place in the eyes of Catholic theology. Now we could talk about the quality of life as we never could before and see clearly our human and Christian duty to promote that quality of life.

God meant us to grow scientifically, technically, ethically, personally, and socially—in thought, in love, in skill, in motivation, in compassion, in sharing and in service. At first sight this view may seem too simplistic and optimistic. It is not so. Whatever interpretation one may place on original sin, the acceptance of growth—of evolution—is necessary for the recognition of evil. For where there is growth, there is imperfection; and where there is imperfection, there is inevitably malfunction; and, ethically speaking, malfunction is sin. The imperfect man cannot avoid sinning. For all that is given to him in creation and redemption, he should endeavor to live above it. But perfection is rare and sin is common.

Dealing with sin in the context of ethical considerations and the fostering of moral values is an integral and important part of the promotion of the Quality of Life. Living in the midst of an enormous transformation in ethical outlook and civilizational clashes has introduced a body of information regarding the human person—our intellectual, psychic, emotional, and social experience—of such magnitude as to challenge radically the pertinence of the concept of Natural Law. While down to Vatican Council II, the church's moral theology tended to be a set of rules concerned with distinguishing mortal from venial sins and prescribing the elements of a virtuous life, the great revival of scripture studies under Pope Pius XII and the Council reestablished the fact that Jesus had taught a morality of ideals, of being perfect as the heavenly Father is perfect, with love as the supreme value.

While natural law ethics meant that, by reflecting on our makeup and characteristics we can arrive at conclusions as to how we should behave, we still face a snag in that our understanding of our nature and characteristics depends on the philosophy prevalent at any given time and the amount of anthropological information then available. The church, since absorbing the philosophy of Plato and attempting to combine it with an evangelical or gospel ethic, frequently found itself inadequate to the demands of the age, as in its inability to condemn slavery, torture, and warfare, and in its current struggle over the morality of nuclear weapons and of the death penalty.

It is no easy matter to arrive at definite conclusions about what the natural law prescribes amid the complexities of modern life. Even Aquinas admitted that while the discernment of good and evil in general is fairly easy, once the problem of particulars surfaces, great difficulty arises. Much disarray in Catholic moral teaching is due to this factor, the challenge of coming to grips with the massive increase in knowledge about ourselves in the multiple dimensions of our being, our activity, and our social evolution. Having rehabilitated creation, we have to take the consequences in what we discover about its mysteries, especially in relation to the human person.

It is to this situation that we owe the trauma of *Humanae vitae.* Pope Paul VI, maintaining the traditional teaching, asserted that "the church, calling men back to the norms of the natural law as interpreted by her constant doctrine, teaches that each and every marriage act must remain open to the transmission of life." Those who find an intellectual argument with this assertion argue that the natural law is not so clear when one takes into account the whole human situation with its biological, psychological, domestic, social, and economic complexities. What has emerged from the debates following the promulgation of the anti-contraception rule is the conviction on the part of a large proportion of the church's moralists that Catholic ethics must give due place to a consideration that traditionally does not seem to have received enough attention, namely, that in complex human situations there can be a conflict of moral values in which the choice must be left to the conscience of the individual.

This conviction has run up against the opposition of the current pope who in his encyclical *Veritatis splendor*, as well as in the Vatican's decisions on many moral—particularly medical—matters, insists that there are absolutes in the field of ethics that cannot be nuanced. Such, for example, is the pontiff's constant condemnation of artificial contraception in which he opposes the secular wisdom concerned with the dangers of overpopulation on both a family and a worldwide horizon. On the other hand, the pope's record in world affairs on the political as well as the religious plane has been exemplary. In some ninety voyages that literally touched on every portion of the globe, he has made an attempt to preach a gospel of political, economic, social, and individual responsibility, while striving to make contact with the world's religious and intellectual leaders. In a final analysis he is credited with having played an important role in the overthrow of the communist system.

In the past the church has had to develop its teaching on important issues such as slavery, the Inquisition, torture, and usury. Pope John threw out the pseudo principle that "error has no rights" which had been used down the centuries to justify the condemnation of non-conformists. The pope maintained that only persons had rights and those rights had to be respected even if the person was in error.

At the same time, while condemning a political or social system because it was atheistic in conception, one could deal with its actions in everyday activities. Both these principles brought him considerable grief and criticism. Nevertheless, in his two great encyclicals, *Mater et Magistra* and *Pacem in Terris*, he laid down principles for the Christian way of life in the twenty-first century.

Meanwhile, the church's thinkers are confronted with the realization that corporate or social ethics have their problems. Corporate ethics refers to the moral issues that affect people, with special reference to their social and political groupings. Thus far the church has not been able to come to grips with the reality of social habits and the part they play in producing and perpetuating evil. People socialized and fossilized in their group attitudes find it almost impossible to change. If the group is a dominant one, it blinds its members to the cruelties and injustices it inflicts, and it reacts with animal ferocity to threats to its identity and position, as is so horribly evident at the moment in the Balkans and the tribes and nations involved with Rwanda. Individuals within one group may be quite humane on other scores, but on issues affecting their group they are beyond reason.

Thus the pope's frequent reference to the similarity between our own age and the age of the early church martyrs expresses a reality. Likewise, his passion for the canonization of saints both ancient and contemporary, people of all ages, education, and positions in life contributes directly to the church's care for the quality of life.

Amid the tremendous revolution within every aspect of the church's life, the conversion to a creational theology in which the splendor and glory of life with the risen Christ has replaced the vale-of-tears concept that prevailed during much of the church's history, we are apparently on the threshold of an explosive religious and cultural advance in which faith will provide the motive and frame of reference for artistic, scientific, and technological commitment.

Given his appreciation of the secular wisdom, buttressed by his call for the sacred charisms, John Paul's attitude toward this world is not easy to evaluate. There can be no doubt that his successor will be confronted with a plethora of issues whose unraveling will require an exceptionally astute intelligence and a theological awareness of extraordinary abrasiveness. Unless of course, the next pope, imitating John XXIII, inaugurates a truly ecumenical council that would include representatives of all the major Christian bodies or churches, with the leaders of the Moslem sects and representatives of the world's religions as observers. With an estimated one billion faithful on its registry, the Catholic church simply cannot continue to avoid taking responsibility for the world's demographic situation.

Quality of Life will then mean human development seen as a contribution to God's overall plan, and human development will embrace every aspect of our multiple roles as human persons: as mystics, as artists, as philosophers, as scientists, and as technicians, as well as in our personal domestic and social involvements.

In a reverie concerned with the papal prophecies of Malachy, the twelfth-century Irish archbishop of Armagh, Carlo Maria Martini, the cardinal of Milan, suggested that the final two prophecies—*De gloria olivi* and *Petrus Romanus*—may have an authentic relevance today. The cardinal sees the original sin of the primitive church in the schism between the foundational Judeo-Christian community of Jerusalem over against the church in exile in Rome. He postulates that the evils in the teaching and practice of that primitive experience are responsible for the failure of today's church to solve its problems within the social and political order, as well as with the body, with sex and the family.

The cardinal sees in the *De gloria olivi* the entrance of the next pope into Jerusalem amidst a joyous palm-scattered reception similar to that given to Jesus on his entrance to the Holy City; this to be followed by the return of "Peter to Peter" in Jerusalem. For all that this is a reverie, it gives some foundation for John Paul's mystagogic proposals for the year 2000. It should enable the penultimate pontiff to delve deeply into the Hebraic tradition of a creational theology as expressed in Genesis and the Psalms.

In the final analysis, the determination of the Slavic pope to enter the promised land of the twenty-first century can only be substantiated by divine providence. With fairly good reason John Paul feels himself a man of destiny.

In a final exhortation regarding preparation for the millennial Jubilee, Pope John Paul advised: "The term Jubilee speaks of joy, not just an inner joy but a jubilation which is manifested openly, for the coming of God is also an outward, visible, audible, and tangible event as St. John makes clear (1 Jn 1:1). It is thus appropriate that every sign of joy at this coming should have its own outward expression. This will demonstrate that the church rejoices in salvation. She invites everyone to rejoice and she tries to create conditions to ensure that the power of salvation will be shared by all. Hence the year 2000 will be celebrated as the Great Jubilee."[1]

Notes

1. "Israeli radice sancta," in *Vita e Pensiero* (Milan, 1993).

8

Papal Social Teaching Today and Tomorrow

ANA MARÍA EZCURRA

The development of Catholic Social Doctrine as a body of systematic thought began in the second half of the nineteenth century, its first formal expression being Leo XIII's *Rerum novarum*. Later popes made regular statements on the subject and gradually built up what has become a Roman magisterium containing additions and changes while maintaining certain positions relatively unchanged.

At the same time, the configuration of this magisterium reflected its links to capitalism, modernity, and socialism. As a result, these three fundamental ties have defined the essential and decisive positions of papal social teaching right up to the present time. This is still true of Pope John Paul II, whose papacy has known a cycle of historic changes that are remarkable for their depth, speed, international impact, and comprehensive reach. Specifically, it has coincided almost exactly with the arrival and expansion of the neoliberal paradigm that produced decisive transformations in the functioning of world capitalism in the 1980s and 1990s.

An examination of some general (and partial) distinctive notes of the social teaching of John Paul in the light of these ties, stressing in particular the links to capitalism in the context of its neoliberal version, will lead to an analysis of some challenges for the future of the church and the papacy in a time of rapid global change.

A SOCIAL DEBACLE OF PLANETARY SCOPE

Since the early 1980s, a profound and sustained increase has occurred in the volume and intensity of global poverty, especially in the South. That process has continued in the 1990s. Even the World Bank recognizes that during the first half of the 1990s progress on this issue has been "modest."[1] In consequence, the population with a per capita income of "one dollar a day or less" declined slightly from 30.1 percent in 1987 to 29.4 percent in 1993, while the absolute number of poor people (defined by the dollar-a-day formula) continued to rise (from 1.22 billion in 1987 to 1.31 billion in 1993).[2]

In addition, a sharp increase occurred during the 1980s and 1990s in inequality within national societies, but also internationally—to the disadvantage of the poor countries of the South.[3] This is a decisive variable. Inequality constitutes the principal structural and determinative factor in the growth of the number of poor (classified as such by the usual measurements). This process, in addition, has produced (and stimulates) acute processes of pauperization in large segments of the population, in particular among the middle classes, many of whose lower sections are now close to the poverty doorway.[4]

Another characteristic of the 1980s and 1990s has been the consolidation of powerful exclusionary processes on a global scale, producing unemployment and subemployment that have become structural, massive, and progressive. The trend is by now also seriously affecting countries of advanced capitalism. The exclusion even affects entire countries that are being left on the margins of world commerce, for example, sub-Saharan Africa.

This social debacle was energetically denounced by John Paul II from the outset of his pontificate. Following Paul VI's lead, he did not hesitate to describe the panorama as serious and depressing, and as an intolerable injustice whose global dimensions he frequently emphasized.[5] That was why he repeatedly insisted that the phenomenon of poverty must be given priority treatment as a matter of social and international justice.

Since the mid-1980s the South's poverty and inequality are arousing a striking concern in a steadily increasing number of multilateral organizations. Even the Bretton Woods institutions, the principal mechanism for the global implantation of the neoliberal paradigm, have noted the problem, albeit belatedly. The World Bank also has adopted a leadership role. Since 1990, it has actually been urging that the top priority of international policy—and of the World Bank itself—should be concretely the reduction of global poverty. It even proposes ad hoc revisions of policy, as other United Nations agencies do.[6]

This recent emphasis on poverty and inequality involves, nevertheless, very different diagnoses and strategies, even some that are contradictory. A central question, in consequence, is to determine how the problem is defined and what is the proposed solution.[7] This applies equally to the social teaching of John Paul II.

THE ISSUE OF CAPITALISM AND PRIVATE PROPERTY

John Paul II has referred more than once, and in formal statements, to "the human deficiencies of capitalism."[8] At the same time, *Centesimus annus* (1991), the first encyclical after the fall of the Soviet bloc, wondered whether capitalism after the collapse of communism could be considered a "model" for the countries of the South. While pointing out that the answer is complex and depends on what we mean by capitalism, he nevertheless gave an affirmative answer if capitalism is understood as an economic system that recognizes the fundamental and positive role of business, the market, and private property.[9]

This is undoubtedly a major innovation. Ever since the time of Pius XI, one of the most constant guidelines of social teaching was the distinction of two "systems" or "ideologies," that of "liberal capitalism" and that of "Marxist collectivism," with the church claiming to hold a position that was aloof and critical of both.[10] The assertion was that the church did not choose.

What is certain, however, is that the Vatican's position was not equidistant from both. It judged—and judges—liberal capitalism as reformable, an attitude that assumes and implies that capitalism is not of its nature to be condemned (while collectivism would be). Pius XI formally embraced that position in *Quadragesimo anno*, 39 (1939). In other words, what the Vatican usually condemned were the abuses of liberalism but not capitalism as such.

John Paul's open acceptance of capitalism by opting for it as a "model" represents, in consequence, an innovation, but one that fits within the tradition of the social teaching. At the same time, this innovation has occurred precisely at the historical juncture of the global expansion of the neoliberal paradigm that is creating an effectively worldwide capitalist system, even if that system is not yet fully in place.[11] Statements like that of John Paul backed by the authority and influence of the Holy See are objectively functional for this process, and they give credibility to what is now the dominant discourse, namely, that there is no other road, no alternative.

The papal social teaching, of course, had always validated capitalism, implicitly or explicitly, because from *Rerum novarum* onward, it gave legitimacy to private ownership of the means of production (capital as a form of ownership) and its corollary, salaried work. Additionally, it constantly defended the existence of a natural right to such ownership, an attitude unambiguously reaffirmed in *Centesimus annus*, 30. The issue is decisive. The attribution of a natural character makes this right universal and not subject to exceptions, which means that a historical regime becomes naturalized and therefore sacralized (since such rights come from God himself).[12]

Capitalist ownership, in consequence, is transformed into an a priori, an axiom. The appeal to the sacred does not make it any less ideological.[13] The result is that the "social question," as introduced by Leo XIII, has always pointed toward the building of a just system,[14] but is always linked to what is conceived as a given and incapable of modification—capital-labor relations. That means that if capital as a form of ownership is inalterable, the corollary inescapably follows: so are salaried work and the nexus between the two. In consequence, justification of capitalist appropriation has, traditionally and expressly, been an option by opposition, namely, against socialism.

At the same time, John Paul declared firmly from the start of his papacy that the right to private ownership of the means of production is not absolute but relative—conditioned by a "social mortgage."[15] In other words, it would have limits arising from another right, that which corresponds to the universal purpose of goods (or the right to common use).

Although the theme of the universal purpose was already hinted at in *Rerum novarum*, it was only with Pius XII that it gained clarity and, above all, preeminence. That is to say, it was elevated to a higher level than private ownership. This emphasis became even clearer in Paul VI and Vatican Council II.[16] The same is true of *Laborem exercens* which criticized "strict" capitalism for defending the right of capitalist appropriation as an untouchable "dogma." In consequence, this encyclical justified the need for adaptations, including processes of socialization and such devices as co-ownership of the means of work (14).

A consistent hierarchization of the universal purpose of goods tends, in consequence, to moderate the rigidity of the axiom that absolutizes private ownership of the means of production. This is evident in *Laborem exercens*, which for that reason dropped the claim of a natural right for that appropriation, describing it simply as a right.

As already mentioned, however, *Centesimus annus* reintroduced the category of natural right precisely at the juncture when, as a result of the collapse of historical socialism, favorable conditions were sprouting for the spread of neoliberal capitalism on a global scale.

The result is the elimination of the previous hierarchization, because the right to common use is overtaken and at the same time restricted by a right that is admittedly inferior, but nevertheless universal, immutable, and, in consequence, limiting. An ambiguous relationship is thus established, a dependent hierarchy: the universal purpose of goods—the primordial objective—is to be attained basically by means of private capitalist appropriation.

This ambiguity revived by John Paul II has significant implications. In effect, by being restricted, the right to common use no longer retains sufficient weight to be recognized as a truly alternative criterion for the historic construction of a new vision of development—a perspective and a task in our view essential.

ECONOMIC LIBERALISM AND THE NEOLIBERAL INFLUENCE QUESTIONED

In keeping with the tradition, John Paul defines liberal capitalism as the kind that defends, precisely, an absolute right of private ownership that would result in an intolerable ascendancy of capital over labor. This form of capitalism he calls illegitimate. Reputed to have originated capital-labor conflict from the time of the Industrial Revolution, it is presented as the principal cause of injustice and exploitation. Following his predecessors, John Paul insists—in opposition to it—on a necessary superiority of labor over capital.

On this issue, accordingly, the voice of the papal corpus—including that of John Paul—is clear; and that is important at this historic juncture characterized by the predominance of neoliberal capitalism and consequently by a veritable onslaught of capital against labor on a global scale.

In *Centesimus annus*, nevertheless, John Paul simultaneously and explicitly identifies the capitalist free market as the most efficient instrument for the allocation of resources and the satisfying of needs.[17] Now, this is precisely the nuclear thesis of the neoliberal theoretical conceptualization and of the neoclassic economic theory. What is more, the main point of the neoliberal program is precisely to install the world market as the primordial mechanism for the allocation of resources both between states and within states.[18]

This support of the capitalist free market does not only constitute another major innovation of John Paul's teaching (one that is added to the explicit option for capitalism). It is further an innovation that is in direct contradiction with the papal teaching's traditional objection to economic liberalism, an objection elsewhere reaffirmed by Karol Wojtyla himself. It consequently introduces another deeply ambiguous element into the discussion, while also representing a regression in papal social teaching.

It reveals, furthermore, the influence of neoliberal thinking which clearly has had and continues to have an extraordinary capacity for ideological penetration, even in parties and movements—whether of capitalist or socialist tendencies—that previously had offered paradigms of development based on the state. The phenomenon can be seen among various Social-Democrat groups in Western Europe, some Latin American parties with a nationalist or populist tradition (such as Peronism in Argentina and the Institutional Revolutionary Party in Mexico), and those responsible for post-Communist economies in Eastern Europe.[19]

In other words, neoliberalism has succeeded in creating a solid hegemony at the level of decision making and on a global scale, and this is probably one of its most resounding successes. It has in fact acquired an enormous intellectual leadership, to the point that the very head of the Catholic church has rearticulated nothing less than its central idea, the one on which the paradigm is built: the intrinsically superior character of the capitalist free market (the best instrument, the one that is most effective for the investment of resources and the satisfaction of needs).

The capitalist market, nevertheless, is not a mechanism of self-regulation that produces the most socially desirable results, as neoclassic thinking claims. Rather, it establishes a political linkage: it gives the victory to the most powerful. In consequence, it is not "free" and leads inescapably to economic concentration. What that means is that the creation of inequality is inherent in its functioning.[20] The neoliberal paradigm thus brings ever more poverty, impoverishment, inequality, and exclusion. Therefore it is not consistent to object to economic liberalism (in the name of social justice), and simultaneously accept its basic principle (which is the cause of this injustice).

THE LIMITS OF THE MARKET, THE ROLE OF THE STATE, AND DISTRIBUTIVE REFORMS

As already mentioned, papal social teaching from its beginnings rejected economic liberalism, and in consequence it condemned uncontrolled freedom of competition. That means that it insisted that the capitalist market has limits. John Paul II reaffirmed this position. What is more, in *Centesimus annus* itself he warned against the risks of an "idolatry" of the market (40), of a "radical" capitalist ideology that "blindly" entrusts to "the free development of market forces" the solution of the problems of exploitation and marginalization (and of "alienation" in the more advanced countries: 42). Here then, we have the outline of a critique of neoliberalism.

Nevertheless, if simultaneously it is asserted that the free market is the best mechanism for assigning resources and satisfying needs, the constitutive thesis of the neoclassic and neoliberal edifice is not only accepted, but also the logical corollary that limitations on the market are inescapably circumscribed and not substantial.

It is pertinent to note in this respect that since the early 1990s the limits on the market listed in *Centesimus annus* began to be more widely recognized and even to have an impact on the neoliberal agenda and, in particular, on the Bretton Woods institutions. In effect, the new hierarchy of poverty opened its door to a relative *aggiornamento* of the neoliberal program that was publicly and systematically announced in the World Bank's 1990 *Report on World Development.*[21] This updating also impacted the area of discourse, producing discussions that tend to diverge from neoliberal orthodoxy. For example, it is now emphasized that there is no dichotomy between state and market, between government intervention and laissez-faire. The functioning of markets is even admitted to be less than perfect, so that the World Bank now recommends some state intervention (though of course "reluctant," careful, and "market-friendly.") Neoliberalism has thus evolved, although hanging on to its primary thesis: the market may show limits, but they do not invalidate its intrinsic superiority. We end up with the concept of *constrained* limits.

As a result, and in the light of what has just been said, to the extent that imperfections (even constrained) of the market are recognized, we face the issue of corrective regulations of these deficiencies, and in particular the issue of the role of the state.

Here, papal social teaching has insisted since *Rerum novarum* that the state has a role in the "social question." That is to say, it did not postulate a state that saw itself as neutral in the capital-labor conflict, but a state that intervenes in favor of the weakest and neediest, in favor of distributive justice.

John Paul reaffirmed this position in *Centesimus annus* (10, 15). This obviously represents a very positive stand in view of the fact that the countries of the South, subjected to the heat of the neoliberal advance, are experiencing an ever greater subordination to the most concentrated segments of international and local capital, and to the multilateral banks. In other words, these countries play a role that is passive but at the same time very active in favor of those segments. What we have here in consequence is a role quite the opposite to that demanded by the tradition of papal social teaching.

In this context, John Paul II gave a real boost to public control of the market, so that he actually judged it in *Centesimus annus* (52) as defining a "social economy" that offers an alternative model to capitalism understood as a system of competition without rules.[22] Public regulation, therefore, constitutes a basic issue by reason of its distinctive and differentiating character. John Paul even takes note of the process of economic globalization, because of which he also calls for greater control of the world market.

Nevertheless, and following papal tradition, he stresses that there are limits to state intervention, and he highlights the all-embracing notion of public control. One of the most persistent elements in papal social teaching is thus the principle of state subsidiarity. It means that in the economic sphere the initiative lies with private agents: individuals first, and then associations. That is to say that he affirms the priority of persons and communities over the state. Concretely, in a capitalist regime this means the predominance of a mercantile form, and therefore a state limited to remedying the defects of the market.

John Paul, moreover, went still farther, introducing in *Centesimus annus* an express criticism of the Welfare State (48), the same criticism that had constituted an axis of the neoliberal paradigm from the outset. Neoliberalism had begun after World War II as "an extreme theoretical and political reaction" against the Welfare State, originally fueled by Friederich Hayek, and then by the Mont Pelerin Society, founded in 1947, which included Milton Friedman and Karl Poppe in its membership.

In the 1980s this original concept evolved into a worldwide program with the same basic focus. It called, accordingly, for a drastic reduction in state activity, and finally for the freeing of market forces and the privatization of every kind of productive activity and services, as well as other key objectives. As a corollary, in the 1980s and 1990s the neoliberal program accomplished the "historic exploit" of dismantling—to a considerable extent—the reform capitalism centered on the state that since World War II had been dominant in countries of advanced capitalism.

To sum up, John Paul condemned welfare capitalism in the name of the principle of subsidiarity, restating in this way another key thesis of the neoliberal agenda. By so doing, he emphasized the limits on state intervention that the papal social teaching had traditionally maintained. Thus, in *Centesimus annus*, 48, he argued that the *principal* role of the state was to guarantee certain protections (to property and individual liberty, to monetary stability, as well as to efficient public services). That is to say that its primordial function would consist in ensuring the fundamental conditions for a capitalist money economy, whereas its role in matters concerning the social question would be more restricted. The capitalist state could not guarantee "human rights in the economic sphere," only look out for them and channel their exercise, since anything more would violate the principle of subsidiarity.

The social teaching of John Paul thus stresses the public control of the market as a key distinguishing note of an alternative model, thereby calling for a state that takes sides in the capital-labor conflict, as his predecessors had done. On the other hand, he simultaneously argues that the state is not the principal instrument for solving the social question.

In other words, he expands the limits that constrain the intervention of the capitalist state, while narrowing those placed on the market. That brings him closer to the "reluctant" and "market-friendly" intervention that organizations such as the World Bank now recommend. That means that the predominance of the mercantile form is increased and the remedial role of the state is reduced, a program fully consonant with the current globalization project of neoliberalism.

NEOLIBERAL CAPITALISM AS A CAUSAL FACTOR IN POVERTY

The serious social deterioration experienced in the 1980s and 1990s forced a widespread questioning of the focus of development. Such concepts as human development and social development even found their way into the lexicon of UN agencies and the international banks. These concepts, however, took on many different connotations because of the divergent answers given to a decisive diagnostic question: what has been the role of the currently dominant model of "market-oriented growth" in the worldwide intensification and expansion of poverty, pauperization, inequality, and exclusion, the role of neoliberal capitalism and its structural adjustments as a causal factor? The answer to this diagnostic question will condition one's attitude to another important question: can free-market capitalism incorporate corrections that will solve these social challenges?

The *aggiornamento* of the neoliberal paradigm undertaken by multilateral credit organizations, especially the World Bank, has also had an impact on the diagnosis. These agencies now admit that structural adjustments generally affect the poor unfavorably, something not admitted by the dominant discourse of the 1980s. But, they add, the effects are short-term and transitional, so that in the medium term the adjustments are consistent with a decrease and even elimination of poverty. They insist that the basic elements of the model are correct, while proposing modifications intended to ease the short-term impact, such as some level of government intervention.

A different evaluation (which we share) is that this social debacle is the continuing result of a prolonged deterioration that began in the early 1980s and still continues, and that it matches precisely the period of the imposition of the neoliberal paradigm. The drawn-out character of the cycle indicates that we are dealing with long-term negative effects that go beyond adventitious fluctuations and are attributable to and inherent in the program. What is needed, accordingly, is a new vision of development, a substantial reorientation that goes beyond corrections of the model and also beyond the proposed changes designed merely to ease its impact.

The social teaching of John Paul also includes an ambiguous diagnosis. On the one hand, and in agreement with previous papal teaching, it identifies the unregulated capitalist market as the primary determining carrier of injustice and exploitation. On the other hand, as a result of neoliberal influences, it supports theses favorable to free competition, in consequence of which an inequivocal identification of neoliberal capital as the causal factor does not emerge.

Ambiguous proposals result. Like his predecessors, John Paul judges liberal capitalism to be capable of corrections that would solve the social question, for example, public regulation of the market. Simultaneously, however, he downplays a key control mechanism, namely, the state, while strengthening the role of the market, thus ending up with a formula that is typical of the neoliberal agenda. He thus imprisons himself within the narrow confines of a corrective strategy that does not challenge the essentials of the dominant system and its economic paradigm.

TOWARD A NEW VISION OF DEVELOPMENT

Calls for a new vision of development, a substantial reorientation that would go further than a strategy to correct neoliberal capitalism, are recently being heard more widely. As the UN Development Program confirms, what is threatened in the South is not the quality of life but life itself. The issue there is survival.

The challenge is serious, both theoretically and politically. So far we have more questions than answers. But there are some contributions that reveal a common line of thinking, even if still general and preliminary.

In particular, there is agreement on the thesis that human (and natural) life should be central to development. That means that human well-being must be seen as the ultimate and exclusive objective of development. It must be the principal and constitutive element, not just something supplementary and subordinated to other objectives such as those of neoliberal *aggiornamento* (economic growth, market profit, and competitive advantage). The question of ends and means is central. The human must always be treated as an end and never simply as a means (an instrument of production, a merchandise) in the service of accumulation and private benefit.

This position, we believe, calls for a break with the concept of development introduced by capitalism, a concept that in the twentieth century also captured some socialists, especially those in the Soviet camp. Franz Hinkelammert describes it as a concept whose underlying assumption is that the maximizing of economic growth based on technical progress necessarily leads to "the humanization of human life."[23] Since the mid-1940s, it was revived and refined by neoliberal thinking, the central objective and primary purpose of which was from the outset to recover economic growth. Even though the *aggiornamento* promoted by the multilateral banks now admits that market-oriented growth is not enough to reduce poverty in the long run, it is simultaneously praised as the principal and central objective.

Without doubt, the centrality of the human demands a radically new concept of development that reverses that belief in accumulation and the consequent inversion of ends and means. Here Paul VI's teaching, especially in *Populorum progressio*, provided considerable input, which John Paul reaffirmed twenty years later in *Sollicitudo rei socialis*. Both popes not only affirmed categorically the centrality of the human, but also began a critique of the dominant concept of development, rejecting and refuting a predominantly economic (and consequently limited) perspective, proposing instead the betterment of the entire human person, a form of development identified as integral. Social inequality—and also international inequality—are consequently incompatible with development. Global justice is affirmed as a right, as is the development of the entire person and of every person, in Paul VI's felicitous expression.

Since the early 1990s, this pioneering stand of Paul VI is gaining ground, to the point that it is central to the concept of human development promoted by the UN Development Program in its annual reports.

John Paul II has dealt with this matter many times. In his first encyclical, *Redemptor hominis,* he adverted to the issue of ends and means, an aspect to which he gave preferential treatment in *Laborem exercens.* This encyclical, like the 1994 Human Development Report of the UN Development Program, rejects the alteration of ends and means that degrades the person as the subject of work. At the same time, the thinking of John Paul, in agreement with some earlier papal statements, seems to put forward simultaneously some theses that are not consistent with a true centrality of the human. This subject is discussed below.

EXPANDED REPRODUCTION OF LIFE
AS AN ALTERNATIVE CRITERION

The market has set itself up as a universal and triumphant criterion for the entire world.[24] It is a fetish and taboo for a conservative wave of support of a worldwide capitalist system. Its highest value is efficiency in cost/benefit relations. This is measured as profit and has as its specific objective market competition. Its corollary is the diminishment of the state's role, and also that of the public, vis-à-vis private enterprise. The result is a massive transfer of income and wealth to the disadvantage of the majorities, leading to a continuous expansion of inequality and an incredible centralization of power in the North and in the concentrated strata of international capital.

Given the seriousness of the situation, what is needed is nothing less than a clear, energetic and unambiguous condemnation of neoliberalism and its effects. Since papal social teaching is weak on this point, we have here a first challenge for the papacy of the future.

If we place human (and natural) life at the center of development, a different kind of reasoning becomes essential, a different criterion that is also universal. What is at issue is a real alternative. Development of the whole person, and of all persons, is incompatible with the neoclassic and neoliberal utopia of the capitalist market as the best way to assign resources and satisfy needs. It is contradictory to attempt both these objectives simultaneously. Yet that is what John Paul attempts. So here is a further challenge for the papacy of the future.

Once we place human (and natural) life at the core of development, then if survival is threatened, the alternative criterion has to be reproduction. This reproduction, however, is not limited to survival, even though this is the immediate and overarching challenge for vast numbers of people. Neither is it limited to what are defined as *basic* needs, even though they remain unsatisfied for ever greater segments of the world's population. Nor are they exclusively material. What is at issue is the recently developed concept of expanded reproduction of life, a concept linked to the principle of the universal destination of goods (focused more on distribution and inequality).

Similar ideas have cropped up in recent years. One is the suggestion of Amartya Sen that has been taken up by the UN Development Program and others.[25] It calls for a forceful expansion of human capabilities, and consequently of human options, by giving people more power over their own lives. This would mean—as the UN Development Program agrees—efforts to ensure a full and all-inclusive blossoming of people's abilities, a thesis in full accord with Paul VI's call in *Populorum progressio* (47) for integral development.

Now, if this expanded reproduction (or similar concepts) is really accepted as the end, no absolute conditions can be imposed as regards means. Ownership of the means of production, for example, cannot be allowed to stand in the way; still less can capitalist appropriation, the foundation of a commercial system that—of its nature—generates inequality. And it is even more illogical to buttress these axioms by appeal to natural and sacred laws. Here we have yet another challenge to the traditional teaching for the papacy of the future.

In the final analysis, it is only when expanded reproduction is truly accepted as the end—without any ambiguities or restrictions imposed by the means—that it can function as a universal and alternative criterion as against any kind of historical regime or criterion of economic organization.

It is true that the banner of distributive justice, with its rejection of inequality, has been a classic element in the papal social teaching. There remains, nevertheless, a challenge: to formulate a clearer analysis of the role of inequality as a conditioning factor of the obstacles that limit the expanded reproduction of life (or the universal destination of goods).

What is here asserted is not only that inequality constitutes the dominant structural vector in the origin of poverty and exclusion, but that it is identified with power relations and, as such, involves a political link. Or, as Mahbub ul-Haq (an assessor of the UN Development Program who helps prepare the annual reports) argues, the true causes of poverty and exclusion are political, so that the focus should be on fighting inequality, a task calling for structural changes in power structures.

A complementary thesis is that such change is impossible without first creating alternative power—the power of the majorities—a position already suggested in the 1993 Human Development Report of the UN Development Program. "Change in the power equation," it said, "requires the organization of a counterforce or even a revolution." To achieve this objective it is important to strengthen civil society, what the report calls "popular participation." This requires a political component with the will and capacity to affect the structures.

It is noteworthy that this thesis, which such agencies as the UN Development Program are now supporting, expresses a nuclear concept from the very beginning of Latin American liberation theology and the Church of the Poor. That is why they have constantly insisted on the creation of a subject (such as "the historic bloc of the oppressed") able to overcome—not merely to condemn—injustice. John Paul II's Vatican has always misunderstood, not to say distorted and condemned, this position by identifying it with Marxist class struggle. The misunderstanding probably results from the papal teaching's problem with dealing boldly with the question of power, and in particular, with admitting that to overcome the dominant model it is necessary to challenge those who are responsible for the tragedy it denounces and condemns.[26] If this is so, a new reflection is called for on the nature of the conflict in the neoliberal stage of capitalist development, a stage which—as earlier noted—involves an extraordinary asymmetry in the distribution of power, in favor of the North vis-à-vis the South and of capital vis-à-vis labor.

On this point, John Paul did recognize "the positive role" of conflict when it is presented as "a struggle for social justice." His teaching, nevertheless, reveals a functionalist matrix. It endorses, not a struggle organized against others, but a conflict directed to a "reasonable accord," one whose rules limit it to a harmonization of positions. Union and conciliation would thus have to prevail always and inescapably, even in conditions of obvious inequality of power—which is the situation in the market—and generally in the capitalist system, an inequality that is accentuated in the neoliberal phase.

Here we have yet another a priori in the papal social teaching that must be changed if we are to attack realistically the central question: what are the conditions that will make possible the historical realization of a new vision of development, oriented—as Paul VI demanded—to the whole person and all persons?

—*Translated by Gary MacEoin*

Notes

1. World Bank, *Poverty Reduction and the World Bank: Progress and Challenges in the 1990s*, Washington, D.C., 1996.

2. Figures for the so-called "developing economies" and "economies in transition."

3. In the introduction to the *1996 Report on Human Development* of the UN Development Program, Program Administrator James Speth points out that, if present trends continue, the economic differences between industrialized and poor countries will be not only unjust but inhuman.

4. Particularly obvious in Latin America and the Caribbean, where the problem of unequal income distribution is extremely serious. The World Bank calls it exceptionally high, the most unequal in the world. See World Bank, *Poverty Reduction and the World Bank: Progress and Challenges in the 1990s*, Washington D.C., 1996.

5. Encyclical *Sollicitudo rei socialis*, 14, 26, 28, 47.

6. For an analysis of the issue, see Ana María Ezcurra, *El Banco Mundial y la cuestión de la pobreza en el Sur*, Buenos Aires: IDEAS, 1994.

7. Adolfo Gurrieri, "Pobreza, recursos humanos y estrategias de desarrollo," in Bernardo Killsberg, ed., *Pobreza: un tema impostergable: Nuevas respuestas a nivel mundial*, Mexico: Fondo de Cultura Económica, 1994.

8. *Centesimus annus*, 33. In the Baltic countries in 1993 he said that such deficiencies refer to the *seeds of truth* to be found in Marxism and Communism.

9. *Centesimus annus*, 42. In this text, John Paul rejects capitalism that does not include public controls on "freedom in the economic sector." He also says that "it might be more appropriate to speak of a business economy, a market economy, or simply free economy." Beyond this question of terms, what seems important is that John Paul accepts capitalism for what it effectively is: a regime in which private ownership of the means of production and a free market constitute the dominant forms of the economic system. Moreover, in 43 he asserts that the church has no "models" to propose, contradicting the choice made in 42.

10. John Paul elsewhere repeated this traditional position, as in *Sollicitudo rei socialis*, 21.

11. See Jeffrey Sachs, "Consolidating Capitalism," in *Foreign Policy*, 98, Spring 1995.

12. Thus in *Christifideles laici*, the post-Synodal Apostolic Exhortation of 1988, 38, John Paul states that the rights of the human person are "natural, universal and inviolable, . . . because such rights come from God himself."

13. This is also an area in which the thinking of John Paul—like much of

papal social teaching—is tinged with ambiguity. The notion of private property refers without distinction to ownership of consumer goods (the right to own what is needed for personal and family growth—*Centesimus annus*, 6) and the ownership of the means of production (which, as such, defines capitalism). Similarly, since the 1981 *Laborem exercens*, the notion of capital refers specifically to the aggregation of machines and instrumental means, that is to say, to a historic form of ownership.

14. As in *Tertio millenio adveniente*, 42.

15. Opening address at Third Conference of Latin American Bishops, Puebla, Mexico, 1979; also in *Sollicitudo rei socialis*, 42. The concept of mortgage represents an advance compared with that of social responsibility found in the traditional papal teaching. See Equipo DEI, "Comentario desde una perspectiva económico-social," in *Juan Pablo II sobre el trabajo humano*, San José, Costa Rica: DEI, 1982.

16. *Populorum progressio*, in which Paul based the teaching on the church fathers, was particularly emphatic.

17. Because of the already mentioned option for capitalism as model, the reference is to the *capitalist* free market.

18. In addition, in *Centesimus annus* John Paul stressed efficiency, economic growth, and monetary stability. These are veritable fetishes of neoliberalism and its model of "market-oriented growth" (15, 19, 35, 48). In addition *Centesimus annus* tends to join both terms in a paradigmatic equation of neoliberal thought. That is to say, the free market is presented as the device that guarantees economic efficiency and growth (its absence having been a crucial factor in the inefficiency and fall of historic socialism: 24).

19. For more on the origins, development, and present influence of neoliberalism, see Ana María Ezcurra, *Globalización, neoliberalismo, y sociedad civil*, Buenos Aires: IDEAS, 1996.

20. This was already pointed out by Paul VI in *Populorum progressio* when he questioned "the basic principle of liberalism" as the rule for commercial exchanges, since in unequal market conditions this brings inequitable results (58).

21. This neoliberal updating has a strategic purpose, namely, to shape an extensive reformulation called "the two-ways strategy" by the Bank. See Ana María Ezcurra, *Banco Mundial y Fondos Sociales en América Latina*. Buenos Aires: IDEAS, 1996.

22. It is not true, John Paul said, that the overthrow of socialism leaves capitalism as the only model of economic organization (*Centesimus annus*, 35), adding that the western countries run the risk of seeing the collapse of "real socialism" as "such a unilateral victory of their own economic system that they need no longer feel the need to introduce the appropriate changes in that system" (56).

23. "La lógica de la exclusión del mercado capitalista mundial y el proyecto de liberación," in *América Latina: resistir por la vida,* San José de Costa Rica: DEI-REDLA, 1993.

24. See Franz Hinkelammert, *El mapa del emperador. Determinismo, caos, sujeto,* San José de Costa Rica: DEI, 1996.

25. See Amartya Sen, *Nuevo examen de la desigualdad*, Madrid: Alianza Editorial, 1995.

26. Jon Sobrino made a similar comment about CELAM's 1993 conference in "Los vientos que soplaron en Santo Domingo," in *Christus*, 3/4-1993.

9

Reformed Church, Unreformed Papacy

JOHN WILKINS

I have not regretted becoming a Catholic. This is now my spiritual family and I love the people who belong to it. I learn from them every day. The church nourishes me and corrects me. But part of the vision which many saw at the time I made my move into the church—shortly after John XXIII's Second Vatican Council—has faded. Perhaps I will not live to see the time when the Spirit renews it.

Some expectations began to be disappointed at the very end of the Council. The mood among the bishops was to declare John XXIII a saint by acclamation, and go home. Paul VI, tentative as ever, demurred. Let John's cause go through the normal channels, he decided, linked to that of Pius XII—two popes of a very different kind. Today both causes are bogged down, and likely to remain so, while that inappropriate connection with Pius XII continues to overshadow John XXIII's project of *aggiornamento*—the updating of the Catholic church.

At the end of the second millennium, Pope John Paul II has governed the Catholic church in the style of Pius XII rather than in that of John XXIII. "I am only the Pope," John XXIII said. And it is significant that when the Second Vatican Council, which he called, was in session, he would leave the other bishops to get on with it, watching the proceedings on television.

But Pope John Paul has always attended the meetings of the Synod of Bishops in Rome, dominating the proceedings in his white cassock. Bishops, I have been told, knew when he was displeased because he

120

would tighten the grasp of his hands on the arms of his chair. That would alarm them, because the Vatican II doctrine of collegiality—that the bishops, with the pope, govern the church as a college in succession to the apostles—has been interpreted by this pope as meaning that the team are being collegial if they say the same thing as the captain. Meanwhile, the curia—the papal civil service—has tended once more to take over the role of the church's central government, whereas in fact its proper function is to be a papal instrument. "The curia treat us as altar boys," one English-speaking cardinal said to me in Rome.

So the Catholic church at the end of the second millennium has been reformed by Vatican II, but is being governed by an unreformed papacy. Will future observers from the vantage point of the third millennium judge John XXIII and his council to have been a blip on the screen of history? Will Pope John Paul II be seen, not as the last pope of the second millennium, but as the first pope of the third?

The Pope from Poland knew by heart in school those verses of the nineteenth-century Polish romantic poet, Juliusz Slowacki, who had predicted the coming of a Slav pope who would be quite unlike Pius IX:

> This one will not—Italian-like—take flight
> At cannon's roar or sabre thrust
> But brave as God himself stand and give fight
> Counting the world as dust.

Karol Wojytyla has a mystical sense of his own and his country's vocation. He saw himself as called to strengthen the church against iniquity. It fell to him, he believed, to reassert integral Catholic doctrine against the corrosive inroads of liberalism and dissent. He set to, confidently, with an iron will.

The command structure at the top of the Catholic church was established by a line of nineteenth-century popes who imposed on it a massive centralization of authority. Recovering from a low point in the eighteenth century, the church in the first part of the twentieth reached a zenith of apparent success and influence. That glittering achievement must never be forgotten. It explains the nostalgia many Catholics feel for that style today, and it would be understandable indeed if some curial cardinals in Rome rejoiced at the "restoration" brought about by John Paul II.

But the cost of that autocracy has to be fully counted. In 1870, under Pius IX—the year of the First Vatican Council—John Henry Newman wrote to a friend, Lady Simeon: "We have come to the climax of tyranny. It is not good for a pope to live twenty years. It is an anomaly and bears no good fruit; he becomes a god, has no one to contradict him, does not know facts, and does cruel things without meaning it." An extraordinary comment to come from so loyal an observer on one of the successors of Peter whose role is to be the "servant of the servants of God."

Besides its command structure, however, the Catholic church exhibits many elements of pluralism. Its popes are elected, its abbots are elected, and for over a thousand years its bishops were elected. It has a diversity of liturgical rites and of spiritualities; its religious orders have fought for and won a relative autonomy, based on the particularity of their vocations; in a number of countries there is a tradition of local discretion in the choice of bishop; and Catholic churches of the Eastern rite have their own Byzantine liturgy, their own canon law, and a married priesthood.

Lessons for the future about autocracy and pluralism can be drawn from the past. It is instructive to compare the reaction of the German Catholic church to Bismarck and to Hitler. The reduction of pluralism in the Catholic church in Germany could be part of the explanation of why, having faced down the former, the church capitulated to the advance of the latter.

Thousands of priests were detained or banned in the Kulturkampf unleashed against the Catholic church in Germany in the 1870s. The campaign was highly aggressive, and Bismarck joined in. But the Catholic church was strongly organized on the ground, with many newspapers and associations, and its own Centre Party. It fought Bismarck to a standstill, and made him seek reconciliation.

In the period of the Weimar Republic and the approaching Third Reich, all this goes into reverse. As nuncio in Berlin, Eugenio Pacelli, the future Pius XII, did not stand aside and facilitate the local church. Instead he intervened. Subsequently, as Vatican Secretary of State, he believed that the way to confront tyranny was through law and the Holy See. He got what he had been seeking when the concordat with Hitler was concluded in 1933, but now the Führer gained a measure of international reputation, and the price was the withdrawal of Catholics in Germany from political and social action. Catholic groups were disbanded, Catholic newspapers closed. Whether or not Pacelli was instrumental in the liquidation of the Centre Party, he was glad to see it go.

Any church order would have been shaken by the totalitarian terror of Nazism. "You try living in times like those," Karl Rahner once remarked. But the question persists why some 20 million practicing Catholics in Germany—one in three of the population—were unable to do more to resist. Part of the answer may be that Rome's support from outside was at the cost of some of the freedom of action of the local church.

Now once more, in the person of John Paul II, there is a pope who towers over the church. It is as though the papal office were on a level of its own, with bishops, priests and lay people subjected to it. The bishops' own voices are subordinate even though they are declared by Vatican II to be themselves vicars of Christ in their own dioceses. This pope is certainly one of the greatest men of the twentieth century, and very possibly a saint. The lives of millions have been touched by him. Saints can be hard to live with, however.

Though the rigidity of the Catholic system must not be exaggerated, the Wojtyla symphony conducted from Rome sometimes seems not so much a blend of sounds and variations on a theme as one note played by many instruments. That makes it harder to listen to. The secular Western world sees John Paul II as a hero, but does not follow his teaching. They warm to the singer rather than to the song.

Yet the song, for those who hear it, is magnificent. "Open wide the doors for Christ. To his saving power open the boundaries of states, economic and political systems, the vast fields of culture, civilization, and development. Do not be afraid. Christ knows 'what is in man.' He alone knows it." In Christ is the truth about what it means to be human; to be contrary to Christ is to be contrary to the truth.

What prevents the song from being more widely accepted? This pope, who was so successful in the first phase of his pontificate—when he shook the rotten tree of communism to such effect—became more pessimistic in the second phase—when he rode out against the permissive relativism of the developed West. Sometimes he has shown his anger. He urged a third way for Poland between communism and capitalism and it was not forthcoming. He hoped that Europe's Eastern half would re-evangelize its Western half and it did not happen.

Catholic believers, for their part, will be modern in their own way.

Many have made up their own minds and have opted for the maximum
of pluralism. Quietly, they have renegotiated the terms of their membership. They widely believe, for example, that the use of contraception to plan their families is licit. They are not going to be driven out of
the church for this reason, although John Paul II has reasserted the ban
on contraception in such strong terms as to suggest that anyone who
infringes it is denying the sovereignty of God.

It is bad for Catholic authority when some doctrines which are ad-
vocated so strongly by the pope are widely rejected. The credibility
gap on these issues is dangerous, and the laity's loss of confidence
extends to the whole hierarchy. People do not expect bishops to speak
their minds on contraception, optional celibacy, and women priests;
they know their pastors have to toe the party line, for otherwise they
will not survive. They see that issues such as the admission of divorced
persons to communion are not allowed to be discussed. Inevitably,
there are those—too many—who leave.

A more pluralistic format allowing a genuinely collegial approach
would make a dialogue about these issues possible. Paul VI's encyclical reaffirming the ban on contraception, *Humanae vitae*, was not a
collegial act. How much greater would have been its authority, Cardinal Suenens pointed out, if it had been—but it would then also have
been different. The initial response to it by bishops' conferences was
pluralistic, each filtering the contents in its own way. But the apparent
opening towards the future was closed progressively by Paul VI and
definitively by John Paul II. It was their judgment that the forces of
pluralism unleashed might shake the church to pieces.

Which way will the popes of the third millennium tilt the balance?
The documents and intention of the Second Vatican Council remain
determinative. If future popes decide to opt for greater pluralism, there
is only one way to start—with the bishops. And if they want to coun-
terbalance the curia, they will have to give collegiality a stronger expression.

That is what the Second Vatican Council did not do. It set out the
doctrine of collegiality in the third chapter of its beautiful constitution
on the church, then left it side by side with the restated doctrine of
absolute papal primacy. As an English interpreter of the Council, the
late Bishop Christopher Butler, used to observe, there was now a moral
obligation on the pope to govern collegially—but he did not have to.

To close the gap between theory and practice, Paul VI instituted the

Synod of Bishops. It was meant to perpetuate the conciliar experience, but has become a rubber stamp. One synod, which stands out as an example, was called in 1980—the first of John Paul II's papacy—to discuss marriage and the family. All the lay couples invited were ardent supporters of *Humanae vitae*, and the synod's proceedings and recommendations were manipulated thoroughly. One or two brave bishops sought to raise the real concerns of their people about contraception and divorce; they awakened no response, and one of the bishops from an English-speaking country who attended was said to feel almost suicidal on the plane journey home. When the papal document subsequently appeared, it could have been written without the bishops ever having gone to Rome; but the pope could now appeal to their "consensus."

Few synods are so unsatisfactory. The treatment of journalists who attend is symptomatic, however. Reporting a synod, one of them has observed, is like trying to eat jelly with a fork. No journalist is allowed in the synod hall while it is in session. Badly translated summaries of the speeches made during the first two weeks are offered; then, when the discussion groups begin, no information is available at all. The propositions drawn up by the bishops at the end are secret, and extraordinary measures are taken to keep them so; leaked copies are urgently perused for evidence about which sensitive subjects have been excised from the list by magic hands in the final stages. Synods should be great moments of teaching for the whole church and for the world; they are not.

There will come a pope who will make changes. But how can he proceed without breaking up the church? An ultramontane liberal could do what is necessary, but then there could be the same polarization—only in the opposite direction—as with Pope John Paul II who has governed the church from the right. The risk of still worse division, when he is no longer there to hold the ring with his remarkable and charismatic personality, is high, and sometimes one wonders whether this pope who feels so responsible to God for the church has felt also as responsible as he should to the church for its future. To outside observers, the Catholic church in the United States seems one of those which has particularly suffered. Some of us rubbed our eyes with disbelief when the late Cardinal Joseph Bernardin, Archbishop of Chicago, unveiled his "Common Ground" project pleading for the two wings to come towards the center for dialogue, only to be attacked for his proposal by a battery of his fellow American cardinals.

A reforming pope could not survive if he set out to do everything himself, nor should he try. He would need to enlist the bishops' majority support, and rest on this power base. Where might he begin? The key is the Code of Canon Law, the instrument of centralization in the hands of Eugenio Pacelli. In helping to draft the code, the future Pius XII knew exactly what he was doing when, for the first time, he claimed that the right to appoint all bishops everywhere belonged to the bishop of Rome in virtue of the primacy he exercised. Until the nineteenth century, by contrast, the appointment of bishops was left, in the vast majority of cases, to the local church.

A canon which is comparatively recent and breaks with tradition could obviously be revised. A reforming pope might first announce that he was convening a gathering of the senior metropolitan archbishops to help him work out how to give the Synod of Bishops a more deliberative function, with careful safeguards to preserve his own position. "I need help," he might say; "after all, I am only the Pope. I cannot, like Atlas, take the whole world on my shoulders. To strengthen myself, I have to strengthen my brothers. They must enjoy fully the say in the government of the church which the Second Vatican Council allotted to them. The Catholic doctrine of collegiality must become Catholic fact. Henceforward, executive authority must be shown by structural expression to belong not to the pope and the curia, but to the pope and the synod."

He would go on, of course, to pay a well-deserved tribute to the devoted work of the curia, without which—whatever radical changes may have to be made to it, especially if there is ever prospect of reunion with the Orthodox—no pope could fulfill his function.

Such a move would receive massive support from the world episcopate, including the most conservative members. There would then be no difficulty in revising the canon which reserves all episcopal appointments to the pope. A commission of canon lawyers could be instructed by pope and synod to suggest a range of forms for appointment to the episcopal office appropriate to the local churches. No candidate could take up office until confirmed by the bishop of Rome, who would also reserve the right to appoint bishops for churches under persecution.

Perhaps there might even be a return to a process by which the people would play a significant part in electing their bishops. Such a move would be hugely popular among the Catholic people upon whom, in the last resort, the church depends (as Newman said, it would look pretty odd without them). The American priest-sociologist Andrew Greeley was startled at the results of a recent survey he conducted of lay opinion in six pilot countries—Spain, Ireland, the United States, Italy, Poland, and the Philippines. Unexpectedly, Ireland and Spain emerged as the most reform-minded, while of the seven measures offered for comment—ranging from the appointment of bishops to married priests and women's ordination—the one which secured majority assent in every single country was the election of bishops. Greeley considered this "remarkable" because, as he pointed out, it is not as yet an item on any church group's agenda for change.

This would be only the starting point. It would be no gain if bishops started behaving like ultramontane popes in their own dioceses. They would need in their turn to deepen their collegial relationship with their priests and lay people, actively encouraging the public opinion in the church which Pius XII said was essential. They would need to free theologians to develop pluralistic approaches in keeping with the scope of their endeavor, which, since Vatican II, is as wide as human experience itself. As the Council's constitution on the church in the modern world, *Gaudium et spes*, put it: "The joys and the hopes, the griefs and the anxieties of the men and women of this age, especially those who are poor or in any way afflicted, these too are the joys and hopes, the griefs and anxieties of the followers of Christ. Indeed, nothing genuinely human fails to raise an echo in their hearts." The vision of Vatican II is of a people's church on pilgrimage with humankind.

That reaffirmation of Christian humanism implies particular theologies to meet particular situations. It implies inculturation—the earthing of the gospel in particular cultures. But when liberation theology sprang up in Latin America in answer to the needs there, it was checked or outlawed from the center—the two instructions from Rome deployed a range of arguments against it, and there was of course a case to answer. But as a result, Pope John Paul II's preaching in the Third World was not able to seize the moral and intellectual high ground it had secured in Eastern Europe. He did not have a word of similar power for the poor of the Third World. The liberation theology he had developed for the Second World, by taking Marxist concepts, such as alienation, and turning them against Marxism itself, was not transferrable. The Third World had developed its own liberation theology, but

he could not use it. When he went to El Salvador in 1983, he praised
the murdered Archbishop Oscar Romero as a diligent pastor and prayed
at his tomb, but could not affirm him as a martyr.

The reforming pope I have posited in this chapter would know that
his collegial move would also kick-start the stalled ecumenical process. *"Ut unum sint"* breathed Pope John XXIII as he lay dying, and
that same prayer that all may be one became the title of John Paul II's
1995 encyclical on ecumenism. The Catholic church's deep commitment to ecumenism is today not in doubt; it breathes through every
page of *Ut unum sint*, which contains an extraordinary invitation. Paul
VI knew that the papacy, while part of the answer to the ecumenical
challenge, was also part of the problem, and Pope John Paul II knows
it too. *Ut unum sint* goes so far as to invite "church leaders and their
theologians" to assist in finding a "way of exercising the primacy"
which will enable it to be recognized by all as "a service of love."

The blunt fact is, however, that unless the Catholic church is governed through a collegiality which is structurally safeguarded, no Orthodox, Anglican or Protestant church will take a single practical step
towards unity with it. The right speeches will be made—and it is important that they should be. There will be meetings and assemblies
and above all there will be joint prayer. All this is indispensable. But
action will not follow.

I can well understand that there would be those in Rome who would
have great doubts about this imaginary pope's reforming program, just
as they had about Pope John XXIII's calling of a council. They have
seen ideologies come and go while the church remains. What need is
there, they would ask, as they asked in Pope John's time, for the church
to be "updated"? Why open windows to the modern world; you never
know what may fly in.

Ever since Pius IX famously declared in the Syllabus of Errors in
1864 that the papacy had no need to reconcile itself with "progress,
liberalism and modern civilization," the Catholic church has been strug-
gling with the question of whether to be modern, and if so, how. The
modernist crisis of the early years of the twentieth century, when the
efforts of Catholic intellectuals to reconcile Christian faith with modernity were rejected as heretical, is not over. There have been some
surprising developments, however. Having previously condemned religious liberty as a "most pestilential error," the Catholic church ac-

cepted it at Vatican II, and it became central in the preaching of Karol
Wojtyla as a weapon against atheism; while in his pontificate, the Catholic church has emerged as the greatest defender of human rights. When
he visited Rome after the Second Vatican Council, the eminent civil
rights lawyer, the late Paul Sieghart, told me he was overjoyed to discover that "this ideal of the French Revolution is alive and well in the
Vatican." There are too many theologians and others, however, who
feel that what the church now preaches to the world, it does not fully
practice towards them.

More surprises of this sort could be in store. Sooner or later, action
for greater Catholic pluralism seems to me certain to be one of them.
The Catholic church in advanced Western societies might then see
itself not simply as a counter-cultural force, but as called to affirm and
evangelize modern freedom.

Modern industrial societies are themselves engaged in a project of
pluralism which is new. From a plurality of races, religions, philoso-
phies and lifestyles, they are trying to construct civic cultures which
give equal rights to all, within the rule of law. The basis is a universal
respect for human beings because of their unique dignity which entails claims about how they should be treated. This is a profoundly
ethical endeavor because it recognizes, as a universal requirement, the
duty to one's neighbor.

But everywhere the viability of these modern societies is threatened by relativism. The idea that no group has a determinative place,
but all must share, can be easily subverted by the idea that no position
or lifestyle is better than any other. For relativism, there are no absolutes. Where pluralism is a debate about how one ought to choose,
relativism merely affirms the fact of choice.

The Catholic church can practice pluralism without relativism. It
already does. But there should be real subsidiarity—decisions should
not be taken at a higher level than necessary. There should be greater
trust and confidence in lay people. There should be no place in the
church for any climate of fear. But an unreformed command structure
will always emphasize an ethics of control rather than one of responsibility. It will start from the hierarchy and end with the people, instead
of the other way around, as the Council did. In assessing the claims of
truth and freedom, it will tend always so to draw the boundaries that
freedom comes off worse. There needs to be greater internal freedom

in the Catholic church. Then it could evangelize the world's freedom more effectively.

***

When in Rome I always try to visit the tomb of John XXIII in the crypt of St. Peter's. It is, appropriately, less grand than the patrician monuments around it. It has the common touch. But the tomb also seems to me to have a somewhat neglected air, as though those in authority felt perhaps a certain embarrassment about the Reformation Roman-style which Pope John initiated, and do not much want to be reminded of it. I hope that one day there will be no reticence, and that John will be raised to the altar. Where Pope John Paul II can be seen as the Rock, John XXIII was the Fisherman. He trusted the Holy Spirit utterly in the church and in the world.

10

The South Will Judge the North

The Church between Globalization and Inculturation

PABLO RICHARD

In the light of the words of Christ, this poor South will judge the opulent North. The poor peoples and the poor nations—poor in different ways, not only for lack of food, but also deprived of freedom and other human rights—will judge those who steal these goods, accumulating for themselves an imperialist monopoly of economic and political domination at the expense of others.

—John Paul II[1]

TWO CONTRASTING PARADIGMS: GLOBALIZATION AND INCULTURATION

The Third World was born with the process of colonization. The colonial expansion of the West in Latin America, Africa and Asia was from the outset a global process that was ethnocentric, authoritarian, patriarchal, and destructive of nature. The global spirit of the Spanish conquest of Latin America was expressed in readily understood words by a Spanish author of the sixteenth century. "It is just and natural," wrote Juan Ginés de Sepúlveda, "that prudent, upright and human men exert mastery over those who lack these qualities. . . . [In consequence,]

131

the Spaniards rule with perfect right these barbarians of the New World who in terms of prudence, intelligence, virtue and humanity are as far beneath the Spaniards as children are beneath adults and women beneath men, the difference between them being as great as that between savage and cruel peoples and peoples of the most exquisite clemency . . . and, I had almost said, as between humans and apes."[2] In another context, Ginés de Sepúlveda develops additional comparisons: "It is natural and just that the soul dominates the body, and that reason presides over appetite . . . and that is why wild beasts accept being tamed and subject themselves to the control of man. For the same reason, the man exercizes control over the woman, the adult man over the boy, the father over his children, that is to say, the most powerful and most perfect over the weak and imperfect."[3]

These texts present for us very clearly the global paradigm of colonial domination. We can formulate it in the following coordinates:

| *Spanish:* | Man | Adult | Human | Soul | Reason |
| *Indian:* | Woman | Child | Animal | Body | Appetite |

This global paradigm of the conquest identifies the domination of the Spaniard over the Indian with the domination of the man over the woman, with that of the adult over the child, and with that of the human over nature. It emerges clearly that ethnocentrism follows the same logic as androcentrism, authoritarianism, and a kind of anthropocentrism that is oppressive of nature. The schema is set out as just and based on the natural law.

The most important element in this paradigm is the identification of all the dominations with the supremacy of the soul over the body and of reason over appetite. The Spaniard, the man, the adult and the human represent the spiritual (the soul) and the rational (the reason); the Indian, the woman, the child, and the animal are only body and appetite. There is consequently a denial that spirit and reason are present in the Indian, the woman, the child and in nature.[4]

In this Western and colonial paradigm we are provided with a perfect justification for the destruction of the indigenous, but also for the destruction of the woman, the child, nature, and the very body itself. The paradigm remains in force right down to the present day, and it is the same logic that is to be found in all ethnocentric, androcentric, authoritarian, and spiritualist dominations that are destructive of nature and of the body.

In our modern times we observe the growth around the world of a new system of globalization that is today based on the concept of total market, a system that seeks to incorporate the entire globe in a new international order. This system of globalization does indeed have some positive aspects, but its asymmetrical, ethnocentric, patriarchal, authoritarian character is evident, as well as its exclusion of the poor and its destruction of nature. This system of globalization is being imposed on the Third World with a high proportion of social exclusion and a devastating destruction of nature.

The crucial issue of inculturation introduced itself from the very first days of colonization. Many missionaries, as well as some indigenous thinkers, offered inculturation as an opponent of colonization. Inculturation was identified as the defense of life, especially the endangered life of the indigenous peoples and of nature. Inculturation not only defended human and cosmic life but, in addition, affirmed the presence of the Spirit precisely where colonization denied it: in the Indian, in the African slave, in the woman, in the body, and in nature. The defense of life and the affirmation of the Spirit in that life led to a radical defense of the cultures of those who had been conquered and excluded by the colonization. Cultures were what identified and sustained peoples and communities whose life and spirit were threatened. Inculturation was consequently identified from the very beginning as the defense of life, of the spirit and of the cultures of peoples who were oppressed and excluded by the globalization of both colonial and modern times.

Inculturation took a stand against destructive and excluding globalization, but it did not reject the universality of the humanity and the catholicity of Christianity. A comment of Pablo Suess is particularly pertinent: "Globalization in the different social domains threatens local and cultural identities. The purpose of inculturation is to strengthen these threatened identities and articulate them. Inculturation does not mean to take refuge in an ethnic and social microstructure, but rather to create universality through the building together of small units that have been strengthened in their identity and rendered capable of creating combinations within a framework that makes global transformations possible."[5] Every kind of colonization and globalization that is excluding is, by definition, not universal. The colonial conquest of the West and the modern globalization of the market are contrary to universality and catholicity. Only the defense of life, of the spirit, and of the cultures of excluded peoples, has the dimension of universality and catholicity. Oppressed people demand universality and they need the catholicity that Christianity offers them. Inculturation, as a defense of the life of oppressed peoples, is the condition of the possibility of all universality and catholicity.

THE CHURCH BETWEEN INCULTURATION AND GLOBALIZATION

The church has to choose between inculturation and globalization. If the church chooses inculturation, it will necessarily be opposed to globalization. The church is universal and catholic if it chooses inculturation. The universality of the church can only be established in defense of life, of the spirit, and of the cultures of the peoples who are oppressed and excluded by Western and modern globalization. The catholicity of the church today faces the challenge of confronting a tradition that is still alive, a tradition of globalization that is ecclesial, Eurocentric, patriarchal, authoritarian, and hostile to the body.

If Christianity reached the Third World by the path of the expansion of European colonialism, it can only regain its authenticity by the path of inculturation. If colonial and modern globalization traveled from the North to the South, inculturation will travel from the South to the North. Globalization oppresses the South; inculturation judges the North. Inculturation of the gospel, or incultured evangelization, is the great tribunal of history in which the West is called to judgment. In this judgment the church has to be the defender of the life and the cultures of the oppressed in opposition to globalization. The gospel, in the process of inculturation, was never a judge of cultures but their protector. Inculturation also demands that the church be the universal protector of life in this calling to judgment of Western colonialism and the modern globalization of the entire market.

Inculturation, from the very beginning, was not a requirement on the part of the cultures but only on the part of the church. Inculturation demands of the church that it break with the paradigms that are proper to Eurocentrism, authoritarianism, patriarchalism, and the spiritualisms that are destructive of nature and of the body. This entails also a declericalization and a decentralization of the church's own structures. If the church responds to these challenges of inculturation, it will be a truly universal and Catholic church—a church meaningful for the peoples of the Third World. That is why we, in the Third World, have such a deep love for the church.

If the church wishes to respond to inculturation and break with the model of globalization, it has to face—at least in the long term—a profound change in the model of church. Today we make a clear distinction between church and models of church. Models do not exist in a pure form, but to permit theoretical understanding, we describe them here in their archetypal forms. We can identify two extreme models of church: the church-society, structured by a hierachy of power; and the church-community, a communion of communities—the People of God. The process of globalization favors a model of church structured by a hierarchy of power, whereas the process of inculturation demands a model of church that is a communion of communities. We are not talking about distinct or parallel churches, but of different models of church—diverse ways or distinct manners of being the same church. The church-society model, which is a political rather than an ecclesial model, is structured by a descending hierarchy of power which we can describe in the following way: God the Father; Jesus; Peter, bishop of Rome and first pope; the twelve apostles, the bishops, the clergy, and the laity.

In the second model of church, which is more ecclesial than political, the first quality is the reality of the church as the People of God organized in a communion of communities. Here also we recognize a hierarchy not at the summit of a structure of power, but in the center of a communion in which God is lived and named as Trinity, a community of three divine persons.

The church as a sociotheological structure of power finds its natural place in an authoritarian and androcentric model of globalization and domination. By contrast, inculturation is possible only in a church that is People of God, a communion of communities, a church in which the participation of all women and men—especially the outcasts of society—is possible and basic.

INSTITUTIONAL CHALLENGES
FOR AN INCULTURATED CHURCH

The Primacy of Peter, Collegiality and the Roman Curia

An inculturated church is not a fragmented or sectarian church. Fragmentation is rather the result of the exclusion which globalization produces. An inculturated church, to the extent that it defends the life of all, is a universal church. The church that accepts and appropriates all the cultures of the Third World, is the only church that is really universal. This universal, inculturated church has greater need than any other kind of church of the primacy of Peter, which in the tradition of the Catholic church is exercised by the bishop of Rome. Here we are not discussing what is essential to the primacy of Peter, only the concrete and historical form of its exercise.[6] The pope himself recognizes the ecumenical longing and the call of the majority of Christian communities to search for "a form of exercise of the primacy that, without renouncing in any way what is essential to the mission, opens the way to a new situation."[7]

Archbishop Giovanni Benelli, while serving as substitute secretary of state to Pope Paul VI, has also made this distinction: "The real, effective power of jurisdiction of the pope over the whole church is one thing. But the centralization of power is another. The first is of divine law. The first has produced many good things. The second is an anomaly."[8] We believe that the primacy of the pope can be exercised in many different ways if we are talking about an authoritarian model of church or about a model of church as a communion of communities.

The pope himself, in *Ut unum sint*, places himself on the side of the latter model of church when he relates the primacy of the pope to the universal collegiality of the bishops: "When the Catholic church affirms that the role of the bishop of Rome corresponds to the will of Christ, it does not separate this function from the mission confided to all bishops, they also being 'vicars and ambassadors of Christ.' The bishop of Rome belongs to his 'college' and they are his brothers in the ministry."[9] The problem arises when the Roman Curia interferes as a third force between the primacy and the episcopal collegiality of the universal church. The primacy and collegiality are of divine origin. The Curia is an administrative reality of human origin. If the Roman Curia assumes a role higher than that of the universal college of bishops, the primacy of the pope is running the danger of following the logic of global authoritarianism. On the contrary, by communion with all the bishops the pope ensures the catholicity and universality of the entire church according to the logic of inculturation. Episcopal collegiality enables the primacy to exercise unity in a church that is inculturated, multi-ethnic, and pluricultural. This exercise of the primacy integrated into episcopal collegiality is more necessary than ever for the churches of the Third World, churches that are threatened by the danger of sectarianization and fragmentation as a result of the process of globalization. The Roman Curia is more vulnerable to the authoritarian process of globalization, and for that reason it should be under the control of the primacy of the bishop of Rome and of his episcopal college. It is the local churches, united to the bishop of Rome, that ensure the catholicity of the church.

In the beautiful words of Saint Ignatius of Antioch: "Wherever the bishop happens to appear, there let all the people come together, in exactly the same way as in wherever Jesus Christ happens to be, there is the universal church."[10] Were the Roman Curia to impose an authoritarian globalization on the local churches, it would destroy the presence of Jesus Christ in the cultures of the whole world and would make impossible the catholicity of the church. Episcopal collegiality, joined to the primacy of Peter, makes possible inculturation and catholicity at the same time. Let us not forget that most of the local churches are in the Third World, and that the future of the church is in the South rather than the North.

Plurality of Ministries and Inculturation

The ministerial structure of the church at the present time follows the logic of globalization more than it does that of inculturation. Ministries are structured in a hierarchy of power within a model of church in which authoritarianism, patriarchalism, and ethnocentricity predominate. Inculturation demands a new ministerial model that has the capacity to evangelize the excluded, and all who live on the periphery of this same system. Inculturation is possible only in a missionary church that stretches beyond the limits imposed by globalization. The social space of the excluded and marginated peoples is a space abandoned today by a church that follows the excluding logic of globalization. The space that the church has abandoned is the privileged location for the activities of the sects, the new religious movements, and the free churches. With its present ministerial structure, the church is incapable of evangelizing the suburban conglomerations of the big cities. A church that follows the logic of globalization is incapable of reaching those who are excluded and marginated.

This logic, however, is beginning to be overcome today by the Christian Base Communities, by the experiences of religious life inserted into the community, by religious movements that arise inside popular social movements, and by experiences of evangelization from inside indigenous cultures that follow the logic of inculturation. The lesson of all these incultured experiences is that we need to reform the entire ministerial structure of the church. Let us hope that this reform is not delayed until too late, namely, when the church has already irretrievably lost the majorities who are excluded and marginalized by the system of globalization.

We are not proposing a change in the ministerial sacramental structure of the church, but merely a reform of its concrete historical forms. The current exercise of the priestly ministry is distinguished by a certain type of academic preparation, by obligatory celibacy, and by the exclusion of women. In sociological terms, quite apart from the theological bases, this confers on the ministerial structure of the church an androcentric, authoritarian, and ethnocentric character based on the logic of globalization. Evangelization, according to the logic of inculturation, requires—and that on a privileged level—the participation of women, of indigenous peoples, of people of African descent, and of all those who are excluded by the system of globalization. The intellectual training, the obligatory celibacy, and the exclusion of women all follow the same logic, which is also the logic that excludes the indigenous, people of African descent, and the poor in general.

Celibacy is not in itself the problem, but only the logic of its imposition as obligatory for the exercise of the priestly ministry, which is the same logic on the basis of which women are excluded. It is a logic that permeates the entire liturgy, including the celebration of the sacraments which are structured according to the patterns of a global, non-inculturated church. The present ethnocentric globalization, in addition, prevents the church from incorporating the people's religious traditions, the myths and rites of their religious faith, and those of their indigenous and African American traditions.

The Power of the Spirit, of the Word, and of Theology

The Third World church finds itself at this point in history extremely challenged, not so much by modernity and secularism as by the process of globalization and its neoliberal ideology. The church that defends the life of all, but especially that of the excluded groups and of nature, is a church that places itself in a position of radical contradiction to the economic, political, and cultural power of the system of globalization. This church, which opts not for power but for the poor, enjoys today in the Third World an overwhelming power that is specific to it: the power of the Spirit, of the Word, and of Theology.

The Power of the Spirit

The church does not have the ability to construct an alternative to the *system* of globalization, but it does have the ability to construct an alternative to the *spirit* of that system. The church lives in the system, but it does not have the spirit of the system. It is not possible to live outside the system, because globalization encompasses everything, but we can live in opposition to the spirit of the system. In the words of Jesus at the Last Supper, as recorded by John, those chosen to be disciples are in the world but not of the world. The system of globalization is not simply what we see and touch. There exists, in addition, inside the economic and political system, a cultural, ethical, and spiritual dimension. Globalization, to the extent that it is authoritarian, patriarchal, ethnocentric and destructive of nature, to the same extent it has a culture, an ethic and a spirituality that is more of death than of life.

The church that defends the life of those who are excluded and does not have the spirit of the system of globalization can construct within the system a cultural, ethical and spiritual resistance to the system itself. The church develops an ethic of life against the system's ethic of death; an ethic of being against an ethic of having; an ethic of solidarity and justice and not an ethic based exclusively on the values of market efficiency and competitiveness; and an ethic in which life is absolute and above the law. The church, finally, lives the spirituality of the God of life against the globalization system's idolatry of death.

The market, science and technology—all good things in themselves—become idols when they are absolutized and present themselves as subjects, gods, or messiahs who bring salvation to man from all evils, including death. As Saint Paul says: "For it is not against human enemies that we have to struggle, but against the Sovereignties and Powers who originate the darkness in this world, the spiritual army of evil in the heavens."[11] We can understand the church that defends life as comparable to that force which, according to Saint Paul, holds in check the mystery of iniquity. The church, as the communion of saints that defends the absolute sacredness of life, would thus be the famous Pauline "obstacle," the thing that "is holding back the ungodly One," and "the Son of perdition," as well as "the mystery of iniquity," all expressions that designate the globalization of death.[12]

The Power of the Word

The church does not live its faith in any kind of way, but according to a canon—a sacred scripture. Every religion has its sacred scripture which constitutes the norm or grammar of its faith. The church believes in one God who speaks and communicates himself. The Bible is listened to as the Word of God, by means of which we are allowed to participate in the divine nature. This Word of God, communicated and listened to, is the highest authority in the church, as Vatican II formally taught.[13] Hermeneutics, the science of biblical interpretation, can be practiced in the church and with different—and even contradictory—understandings, depending on the model of church adopted.

A church of power, structured according to an authoritarian, patriarchal, and ethnocentric logic, will also have a hermeneutics that is consistent with that structure and that logic. The Bible is read with the spirit of the system and it is internally transformed in three different ways. First of all, the Bible is presented as a single and unique canon. A canon that is authoritarian, patriarchal, and ethnocentric is created within the canon. Secondly, the Word of God is identified exclusively with the literal meaning of the text. This happens in the fundamentalist line of thinking in which the Bible is reduced to a letter that kills. Finally, the Bible is interpreted in closed and controlled hermeneutic spaces, within which it is held captive. This happens in some academic areas in which science dominates and suffocates the Word; or in some ecclesial areas in which the magisterium is elevated above the Word of God and controls it. The church—People of God, communion of communities, and apostolic church faithful to the tradition of the Kingdom as preached by Jesus and his disciples—does not interpret the Bible with the spirit of the system but with the Spirit with which the Bible was written, a Spirit in which the Word of God recovers the liberty and authority that are its birthright. This model of church constructs a liberating hermeneutics, not according to the logic of globalization but to that of inculturation. This hermeneutics of liberation seeks to recover the meaning of the Word of God that has been distorted by the three oppressions just mentioned. First of all, it seeks to free the Word of God from canonical oppression, from that canon within the canon that is authoritarian, patriarchal, and ethnocentric. In our time, exegetical studies are reconstructing the extreme variety of historical and cultural contexts within which the Bible was born.

The Bible reflects this plurality of contexts and develops an even greater plurality of theological and ecclesial currents. The biblical canon is the consecration of this plurality and not a unique and absolute canon imposing an authoritarian, patriarchal, and ethnocentric orthodoxy. Quite the contrary. The canon incorporates a spiritual plurality in which the life of all women and men finds a space of legitimacy and authority, a space in which there exists in a very special way a preferential home for the poor, the excluded, women, and the cultures of all peoples. The canon is not authoritarian. On the contrary, it embraces the liberty of the Spirit against the regime of law, sin, and death. Against fundamentalism, the hermeneutics of liberation asserts that the Word of God, already present in the Book of Life, is previous to and higher than the biblical text. It seeks to rescue the spiritual meaning of the Bible, the meaning of the Word of God for our own history, in the light of the text.

Finally, the hermeneutics of liberation seeks to create a space of community meaning in which the Bible is read and interpreted with the sense of faith of the People of God organized in a communion of communities. In this space neither biblical science nor the magisterium is inserted in an absolute way above the Word of God, but as a service to it. The communitarian and believing reading of the Word of God, done in the bosom of the People of God and its communities, needs more than ever the service of biblical science and of the magisterium of the church. This liberating process of the Sacred Scriptures is possible only in a church that follows the logic of inculturation. It is equally the logic of inculturation that constructs a liberating hermeneutics in which the Word of God recovers its liberty against every authoritarian, patriarchal, and ethnocentric logic.

The Power of Theology

Every historic transformation is possible when a theoretical space exists that makes it possible. The rise of a new practice of faith and of a new model of church in the Third World became possible only because of the development of the theology of liberation. In the world of the poor and of the excluded, theology is more necessary than ever, just as the power of the Spirit and of the Word is more necessary than ever before. The theology of liberation is a new way of conceiving the Spirit and the Word in the contemporary situation of the Third World. In the construction of a model of church that responds to inculturation, involving a clean break with the model of globalization, theology is a power and a theory that are absolutely necessary.

In the actual model of globalization, everything is determined by the dictates of the market economy. The national state is called seriously into question by the neoliberal ideology, since it is claimed that it is the role of the market to regulate economic life and national policy. In this new context, political transformation of the system becomes almost impossible. No social group can take political power to carry out a major transformation of society. The world market today absolutely excludes every political liberating project.

For this reason, for the poor and excluded, hope no longer comes through a political process but by an extreme transformation of society from below—from the base. It is not a question of seizing power but of building a new power out of what we now have begun to call civil society, understood essentially as growing out of grassroots social movements, and recognized as movements that create alternatives to the global system of domination. In a word, we are witnessing a displacement from political society toward civil society.

Such is the new historic context of the practice of our faith and of the rebuilding of our hope that has profoundly transformed the theology of liberation. In this new context, theology appropriates new themes—such as culture, gender and nature—in a plurality of theologies of liberation; for example, Indian theology; African American theology; the theology of woman; and the theology that develops in dialogue with economics, with ecology, and with the new issues raised by modernism and post-modernism. We can say in general terms that the theology of liberation is acquiring, at the present time more than ever before, the rationality of inculturation which we have already defined as the logic of a society in which there is room for all women and men, and in which the defense of life—especially the life of the excluded—is posited as an absolute. If the universal church wishes to adopt the logic of inculturation and not that of globalization, it should also adopt the historic power of those theologies that are coming to life today within the Third World.

—*Translated by Gary MacEoin*

Notes

1. Homily at Mass celebrated at airport of Namao, Canada, 17 September 1984.

2. *Tratado sobre las justas causas de la guerra contra los Indios* (Mexico: Fondo de Cultura Económica, 1941), p. 101.

3. Ibid., p. 85.

4. See my article, "Biblical Interpretation from the Perspective of Indigenous Cultures of Latin America," in Mark G. Brett, ed., *Ethnicity and the Bible* (Leiden, New York, Cologne: E. J. Brill, 1996), pp. 297-314.

5. Unpublished article, scheduled to appear in *Senderos,* Costa Rica, 1997.

6. For what follows, see the encyclical of Pope John Paul II, *Ut unum sint,* 25 May 1995; also the public address at Oxford University, England in May 1996 of Archbishop John R. Quinn of San Francisco, California, entitled "The Exercise of the Primacy: Facing up to the Costs of Christian Unity," *National Catholic Reporter*, Kansas City, MO, vol. 33, No. 34 (12 July 1996): pp. 12-14.

7. Quoted by Archbishop Quinn in "The Exercise of the Primacy."

8. Quoted in ibid., cap. IX.

9. *Ut unum sint,* 95. The phrase "vicars and ambassadors of Christ" is from Vatican II's *Lumen gentium,* 27.

10. *Smyrna*, VIII, 2.

11. Ep 6:12.

12. 2 Th 2:1-2. See my book: *Apocalypse: A People's Commentary on the Book of Revelation* (Maryknoll, N.Y.: Orbis Books, 1995).

13. The Constitution *Dei verbum* of Vatican II says that "the magisterium is not above the Word of God but at its service" (10).

11

The Papacy of the Future

A Protestant Perspective

HARVEY COX

In *Ut unum sint* Pope John Paul II reminds his readers that the supreme vocation of the bishop of Rome is that of striving for the unity of Christians. I welcome this historic encyclical and I am especially grateful that the pope seems to have invited all Christians into a conversation about how this quest for unity might be advanced. But how serious is this invitation? We have some reason to be hopeful. Immediately after the encyclical appeared the dean of the Waldensian (Protestant) Seminary in Rome, Paulo Ricca, telephoned the Sacred Congregation for the Doctrine of the Faith and asked if it really meant that non-Catholics were to take part in this exciting conversation. Not only was he assured that we were, but a short time later Cardinal Joseph Ratzinger himself came to the Waldensian Seminary and, before a packed house, discussed the encyclical with Dean Ricca and other members of the faculty. Since then, Vatican officials have participated in other high level discussions on the topic with Protestant and Orthodox church leaders and theologians. I do not believe non-Catholics should underestimate the importance either of the pope's invitation or of Cardinal Ratzinger's demonstration that it is genuine. I do feel, however, that what Protestants could contribute to the conversation might be quite different from what the pope or his prefect anticipate.

No doubt, of course, there will be Protestants, especially those in

the more "catholic" and more ecclesially self-conscious denominations who will be only too happy to take up the old debates about the
validity of orders, what infallibility means, the significance of Marian
piety, maybe even the current status of the *filioque* clause. I will have
something to say about these venerable polemical chestnuts later on,
but I rather believe that everything that could possibly be said about
them has already been said, most of it more than once, and that the
chance of a breakthrough coming on such an agenda is fairly remote.
What attracts me most about *Ut unum sint* is the pope's suggestion
about "leaving behind useless controversies" and his intriguing allu-
sion to a "new situation." Just what is this new situation that makes it
possible to carry on a discussion among all Christians about how the
pope's vocation for unity could best be carried out?

I will not try to summarize the wide array of Protestant points of
view of this topic. They range from those who think that, with a few
modifications in the more recent enlargements of the papal claims, the
bishop of Rome might well be endowed with some symbolic primacy,
to those who continue to feel the whole history of the papacy has been
a calamitous mistake from the start. Then of course there are those—
and there are many—Protestants who are so busy evangelizing Latin
America or just trying to stay alive in China that they rarely if ever
think of the papacy, except maybe when they see the pope on television emerging from an Alitalia jet or waving from his specially designed limousine. I also realize that the questions the other authors in
this volume have dealt with so ably, about the pope's role in the governance of the Catholic church, are crucial ones. But they have discussed
them so thoroughly I prefer to take a different approach. I wish to
enter the very personal observations of one particular Protestant and
to concentrate on my hopes—perhaps even my fantasies—for the future ministry of the papacy to the whole world.

I

I remember well the first time I found out there was such a thing as
a pope. It was in February 1939, and I was nine years old. Walking
down our street in the small town of Malvern, Pennsylvania, where I
grew up, I noticed that the doors and lintels of the imposing, grey-
stone St. Patrick's Church, which stood almost next door to our two-
family brick house and on the same block as the Baptist church we

belonged to, were hung with yards of somber black ribbon. When my father came home from work that evening, I asked him what it meant. My father, the non-churchgoing offspring of two churchly Baptist parents, pursed his lips for a moment before answering. "Well," he finally said, "their pope died. He lived in Italy, but he died, and those are mourning decorations. It's the way they show their sadness."

He may have hoped I would be satisfied with the answer, but of course I wasn't. I wanted to know what a pope was—it was a term I had never heard before—and why anyone from Malvern would be that sad about the death of someone who had lived so far away. He paused and then tried to explain as best he could what the pope meant to Catholics. Sixty years later what impresses me about his reply is how free it was from bigotry or papist-baiting, something I only learned about much later, and never heard at all either in church or at home. My parents' attitude seemed to be that if Catholics, whose ways were a bit mysterious anyway, wanted to have an Italian who lived far across the ocean as the head of their church, that was their business. It had nothing much to do with us.

Like many Protestants, however, I have had a continuing fascination with the popes and the papacy. As I grew, I also came to see that the pope, even though we were not Catholics, did have something to do with us. The pope who had died on that cold February day in 1939 was, of course, Pius XI, the librarian-diplomat, whose memory tends to be overshadowed by his flashier protégé and eventual successor, Pius XII. It was that pope whose somewhat sour visage and rimless glasses I came to recognize during my teenage years as the Italian who headed the Catholic church. I never saw him as a very warm or welcoming figure, but I have also discovered that many Catholics didn't either. Still, as I began to study—and become unendingly fascinated—with history, first in high school and then in college and ever since, I could not help noticing that whatever period or problem I was reading about, the popes were always there. Try to study the history of political institutions, philosophy, art, science, or literature without bumping into popes everywhere. They did, after all, have something to do with us for they were significant actors in a history we all share. Besides, whatever you might say or think of the claims made about the popes, it would be hard to find a more fascinating collection of men (I am leaving out "Pope Joan," whose credentials and historicity, it seems, are still in some dispute). The bishops of Rome have included saints, rakes, scholars, schemers, administrative geniuses, reformers, egomaniacs, tyrants, art collectors, warriors, builders, and even an occasional personage with an interest in theology. Somehow, as I plunged deeper into history, then theology and the history of religion, it was the sheer persistence and virtual omnipresence (for blessing or for bane) of the papacy, that impressed me. I began to see at least a glimmer of plausibility in the hoary Catholic argument that any institution which has survived that long, despite the fornicators and four-flushers who had actually occupied the office, must be taken with some degree of seriousness. If the God of the Bible, as I believe, acts in and through human history, then it has to be conceded that the papacy, and not just in the West, occupies a not inconsiderable chunk of that history.

I was already a doctoral student in the history and philosophy of religion at Harvard in 1958 when Pius XII died and a roly-poly character named Roncalli was elected and took the name John XXIII. His choice of this name was a bit puzzling to those of us who knew a bit about papal history since the previous John, who had reigned seven hundred years earlier, had become a slight embarrassment to the church. John XXII had sat in Avignon and thus represented an episode in church history some Catholics would prefer to forget. He had worried theologians (is anything really new?) by talking about his mystical visions of what would happen after the final judgment. But there you had it again: persistence. The Catholic church had waited seven hundred years, but now seemed an opportune time, at least to Roncalli, to retrieve and refurbish a perfectly good biblical name. It was touching to be reminded by John Wilkins' essay in this volume of something I had read, but nearly forgotten in Peter Hebblethwaite's biography of Angelo Roncalli, that virtually the last words he uttered on his deathbed were, *ut omnes unum sint*. I think it is safe to say that, given Roncalli's short but spectacular papacy, the name John has now been fully restored and vindicated. The Catholic church, it seems, is not in any particular hurry about these things.

John XXIII did far more than reclaim a papal name. He demonstrated, in a thrilling and imaginative way, the kind of freedom a pope has if he is willing to exercise it. John XXIII not only issued encyclicals like *Pacem in Terris* that still reverberate, and not only assembled a council that changed the church forever, he also redefined the religious, cultural, and moral meaning of the papacy itself. He did this, moreover, not through any sweeping juridical reforms but simply by the way he lived. I continue to be astonished when I remember how not only Protestants, Jews, and members of other religions, but also atheists, skeptics, and agnostics seemed to admire and even love him, and how genuinely sad hundreds of millions of people were when he died. I am also somewhat baffled by it. Why should so many people who, like my parents, think of this pope business as an odd but harmless thing Catholics indulge in, have any interest in whether a pope is generous, expansive, humble, or not? It almost suggests that there was, and is, something deep in even the most unpapal (as opposed to antipapal) soul that hopes for a pope we can all feel fond of. It is the evolution of this cultural-spiritual and moral dimension of the papacy that is left out of most of the suggestions I see about the future of the papacy. Maybe the omission occurs because most of those who engage in the discussion are Catholics, and since they tend to be preoccupied with other aspects of the papal office, they might miss this one. Perhaps you almost have to be something of an outsider, and therefore not so wrapped up with issues of collegiality, infallibility, and curial power, to appreciate it.

II

The first pope I met personally was Paul VI. It was at a consultation in Rome sponsored by the Vatican's then newly established Secretariat for Nonbelievers, whose president was Cardinal König of Vienna. It was a meeting that altered forever my ideas about the papacy and about what its future course might be. I was not, however, invited to the conference as a nonbeliever. Vatican II had made it clear that Protestants were now to be viewed in a much more favorable light, and a Secretariat for Christian Unity had just been established. I was invited because it was shortly after the appearance of my book *The Secular City* and someone at the Vatican, possibly even prompted by the pope, thought I knew something about secularization and modern unbelief. When at the conclusion of our talks Pope Paul VI received the scholars who attended, he took my hand and, with gentle eyes looking over his hawk-like nose, told me that he had been reading my book and that although he disagreed with some of it, he had read it "with great interest." I was immensely pleased but also sorry the next day that I had not asked him to put it in writing. It would have made a marvelous blurb for future editions.

What was important about that consultation, however, was not meeting the pope. ("It's like visiting the Statue of Liberty when you go to New York," the monsignor who administered the Secretariat told us before the audience.) The important thing was that this was a meeting sponsored by an official organ of the Vatican curia to which not only Protestants and Jews but nonbelievers and even Marxists were invited. It suggested a vast new arena for papal leadership, a transformation of the Vatican itself into an open meeting ground where representatives of various contending world views could come together for uncoerced and honest conversation. This hope is voiced by Giancarlo Zizola in his essay in this volume when he suggests the possibility of the Vatican becoming "such a point of concentration of spiritual authority in the eyes of all Christians and of all peoples as to become a kind of agent of unification of all forces that tend toward the good, without losing at the same time continuity with what had previously been considered good." This represents a truly catholic vision of what Christ's prayer, *ut omnes unum sint*, could mean.

To my mind, that meeting was a truly remarkable gathering, but I regret to say that the Secretariat for Nonbelievers soon fell upon hard days. Perhaps it was just a little too daring, a bit in advance of its time. Still, I like to think of its courageous work almost as an eschatological sign, a token of future possibilities. After all, the authority of the bishop of Rome in the early years of Christian history arose when he was looked to as the one to hear out and settle otherwise intransigent disputes among contending parties within the church; so the kind of meeting I attended would represent a logical extension of that practice. Someone reported a few years ago that the reason the Secretariat for Nonbelievers has declined into insignificance is because neither Cardinal König nor the people who administered it in Rome were cagey enough to deal with the hardball of internal curial politics. This may well be the case, but again, maybe one has to be a non-Catholic, or at least blissfully uninvolved in the internecine power struggles of Rome, to appreciate just how powerful and promising that historic gathering was. I still believe, despite more recent reverses, that it presages a role the papacy—and quite possibly only the papacy—could play in the next century.

Theologians sometimes use the word "proleptic" to describe those hints and foretastes of the final consummation that are already appearing here and there in earthly human history. The sacraments are such proleptic signs, especially the Lord's Supper. But the church itself is also called to be a sacrament, a "provisional demonstration," as Karl Barth once wrote, "of God's intention for all humankind." A couple of years ago I witnessed just such a proleptic demonstration in Milan, where Cardinal Carlo Maria Martini has created an annual series of meetings in which believers and nonbelievers gather to share insights and opinions about some issue of vital common concern. It is an immensely popular event, drawing tens of thousands of Milanese away from their offices, style shows, and discotheques. Tickets are free but one must request them and they are always in short supply. The year I participated, priests and lay people, scholars and politicians—including the mayors of the four largest cities in Italy—came together to discuss "The City: Blessing or Curse?" Cardinal Martini himself, in full vestments, ably presided over the meetings and made his own comments. Despite film openings, theatrical productions, concerts, and numerous art exhibits going on in the city at the same time, it was clear that Martini's gathering was the one no one wanted to miss. It was "the open church" at its best, a demonstration not only of what the church should be but what, at times, it already is. Its only limitation was that it was a bit provincial. It was Italian, even Milanese. The setting and sponsorship lacked the historic resonance and universal sweep of Rome and the Vatican. John Paul II had taken a couple of initiatives in this direction, such as the memorable prayer meeting for members of the different world religions in Assisi and his historic invitation to the head rabbi of Rome to say Kaddish in the Vatican. What interested me most about these events was how eagerly people responded to his initiative and how grateful they were. The future papacy, it would seem, does not have to be invented out of whole cloth. Strands of it are already in hand. They need only be woven together and spread.

III

The ending of the cold war may be one of the most important features in the "new situation" the pope refers to. But the world is still tormented by divisions, the most painful and salient of which do not run along denominational or even religious fault lines. What separates us today is the way hunger and misery are distributed—or maldistributed—in the world Jesus Christ came to "make one." Thirty years ago, when the Second Vatican Council adjourned, the countries of the

North were roughly twenty times richer than those of the South. To-day, after decades of development programs, loans, aid and marketization, they are fifty times richer. According to the UN Development Report for 1996, the world's 358 billionaires are wealthier than the combined annual income of countries with 45 percent of the world's population. The gap between the hungry and the satiated has never been wider and it deepens every year, something both Ana María Ezcurra and Pablo Richard have forcefully pointed out in their essays. Since nearly two billion of the world's population are Christians—and this includes hundreds of millions of the world's impoverished—it is self-evident that what dismembers and disfigures the Body of Christ today and makes "visible unity" such a painful challenge is not the divisions among churches. It is the chasm between the minority of the privileged and the majority of the poor, sick, and abandoned to whom Christ addressed most of his ministry.

This is not to say that some kind of ecclesial "visible unity" among Christians is not important. It is indeed important, but not as an end in itself. The unity of Christians is vital, but it is instrumental, not ulti-mate. When Christ prayed, in the words quoted in the encyclical, that "all might be one" (Jn 17: 22), he himself recognized this instrumen-tality. He prayed for unity *so that the world might believe the Gospel.* I doubt that any Catholic or Protestant theologian would deny this. But the Gospel we hope the world will believe is about the coming of God's reign of justice which signifies the vindication of the poor and the ingathering of the excluded and forgotten. So the question we need to ask is this: how can the quest for Christian unity, which the pope ac-knowledges is the highest goal of his ministry, be understood as a means to healing the wounds of the nations and overcoming the cruel sunderings that are tearing the flesh of the human family?

IV

This takes me back to the old ecumenical agenda, what the pope refers to as the "useless controversies." I realize these endlessly de-bated questions cannot be set aside completely. But when we recog-nize that the unity of Christians, which the pope says he embraces as the main goal of the Petrine ministry, is a means toward achieving human unity, this casts the timeworn agenda in a new light. It enables us to approach seemingly obsolete questions from a new angle. The stubborn dilemma about valid and invalid orders, for example, might seem less intractable if we kept in mind that the whole church, in all its many twigs and branches and including the laity, is called by God to be a minister/servant to the world, and that the various orders of ministry are principally various forms of servanthood. Several writers in the present collection have already reminded us of this, and it seemed significant to me that John Paul II refers to himself in this encyclical as *servus servorum Dei*. Admittedly in the past popes have not always used this title to signal a readiness for humility and servanthood. Can we hope that this time he may be quite serious about it?

The issue of humility brings up another feature of the papacy which has sometimes been a sticking point in the past: pomp and pageantry. Catholics who have drunk deeply of the fountains of St. Francis sometimes suggest that the palaces and the regalia one encounters around St. Peter's create an unnecessary obstacle to unity. Consign them all to the bonfire of vanities, or better still sell them all and give the proceeds to the poor, they urge, and the separated brethren will flock into the newly trimmed-down bark of Peter.

Not so. I believe most non-Catholics enjoy the baroque and theatrical aspects of the papacy, albeit sometimes a little secretly and guiltily. But there is a reason for this. Ever since the pope was stripped of his earthly fiefdoms in 1870, it is obvious that he is not a king or emperor in the earthly sense. His guards, after all, carry halberds, not uzis (although I assume that since the assassination attempt there are some real bodyguards with real semi-automatic weapons just offstage.) When the pope really ruled over worldly domains, the plumes and maces were a genuine offense. They are not today. But they are not just camp either. Their somewhat operatic staginess reminds us that, in a strange way, the pope does have his divisions, but they consist entirely in the moral and spiritual authority symbolized by the living tradition these colorful antiques recall. The outcome of what Pius IX considered a great catastrophe, the loss of the Papal States in the *Risorgimento*, has turned out instead to be a blessing. It resulted in a papacy that wields more genuine power than it ever did, none of it coming from the barrel of a gun. Maybe next the papacy will discover that its real spiritual power does not come from the barrel of an excommunication notice either.

Also, on the vexed issue of Marian piety, I think a fresh approach might eventually help diminish the rancor and tone down the rhetoric.

The "new situation" that is pertinent here is the worldwide triumph of the culture of market capitalism and the individualistic consumerist mythology that supports it. Is a counter symbology available? Recent feminist scholars have sagely pointed out that the relationship of the mother (or the primary parent) to the child reminds us that the current economic model of human beings as calculating decision-makers who base their choices on rational self-interest leaves out a huge piece of reality. It leaves out most of the relationships we really have, and certainly the most important ones. No one makes the calculated choice to be a child. No child chooses its parents. Parents and children rarely enter into contractual relationships, and choosing to become a parent is rarely a profit-motivated decision. In addition, the child-parent relationship is one in which the power equation changes over the years. One partner begins weak and becomes strong, the other eventually grows weaker and needs the strength of the one who began in total dependency. We should not overlook, as Protestants often have, that Marian piety is often the major devotion precisely of those masses of people who tend to be left out—or pushed out—of the self-interest-centered market culture. Also, the symbol of the parent and child is an immensely powerful ecumenical one. It is a folk icon you can find in almost any home of any denomination. Rightly understood, the place of Mary in Christian spirituality (and not only Christian) could be an asset rather than a liability to Christian unity. At the same time it could serve as a desperately needed counterweight to the pervasive image of the calculating economic decision-maker which provides the basis for the religion of the market with its sacrament of endless consumption.

The other contributors to this volume have already presented convincing arguments about how one might re-think such questions as infallibility and collegiality. Regarding the former, it has always seemed odd to me that the papacy, which has been one of the most stalwart foes of the acids of modernity has inadvertently allowed itself to be taken in by one of the most corrosive of these cauterants—literalism. The very concept of infallibility assumes a view of language and its relationship to God, to persons, and to the world which is highly reductive and distinctly modern. It implies a wooden, even lifeless notion of language, a view which has been challenged not only by the best poets of the century but also by the most insightful philosophers. It is especially surprising that a pope who before his elevation was a respected phenomenological philosopher (and gave a lecture on this subject at

Harvard Divinity School) should be caught in such a contradiction.

Doctrines are of course an essential element in the life of the church, but a deeper and more nuanced understanding of the nature of doctrine—and its kinship to poetry, song, liturgy, and prayer—might eventually make the whole infallibility question moot. But on this question I am afraid that Catholics do not have much to learn from Protestants, who have sunk even deeper into the abyss of literalism. Not only the fundamentalists but also their mirror image, the historical critical zealots who vote with variously colored balls on which words are and which are not the *ipsissima verba* of Jesus, have fallen into the literalist mire. Both have forgotten the essentially mythic and symbolic quality of religious language. It were as though one of the most unattractive components of modernity had taken its revenge on religion by seeping like some invisible but lethal vapor into the inner sanctum of the churches themselves. Maybe at some level the Pentecostals and charismatics have sensed this. For them, language, including religious language in its present debased state, is suffocating faith. Therefore glossolalia seems to be one way to start breathing again. There is a crisis of language in the churches, but the concept of infallibility is a symptom of it, not a cure. It is not for nothing that thoughtful observers of worship have detected a surprising similarity among Quaker silent worship, speaking in tongues, and the Latin Mass.

Protestants may have a little more to contribute when it comes to questions of collegiality. Not that all non-Catholic forms of polity have always worked perfectly. They have not, but there are so many of them that they provide a sort of laboratory, a thousand flowers blooming. And there is no such thing as a failed experiment since we learn from our mistakes as well as our successes. The down side of the "new situation" however is that the modern world has taken its secret toll here as well. What literalism is to doctrine, bureaucracy is to polity. Whether it be a free church, connectional, presbyterial, or episcopal polity on paper, almost all Protestant churches—and Catholic churches as well—have been thoroughly bureaucratized. Does the pope really know or care about what is going on day by day in those anonymous labyrinthine offices that line the Via della Conciliazione? When the buses stop and the traffic lights change, the busy clerical pen pushers who file into those buildings carrying their brief cases look like Xerox copies of their counterparts at Dean Witter or the Prudential Life Insurance Company, except for the clerical collars.

If anything, Protestants seem to have learned a bit in advance of Catholics, that new, de-centralized, more loosely organized forms of polity are urgently required. If centralization, hierarchy, and top-down vertical authority came close to putting IBM and General Motors out of business, why should they work for us? This is hardly a heretical thought. "Subsidiarity" is, after all, a very old and established principle in Catholic social teaching. There is no reason why it should not apply within the church itself. In his thoughtful lecture on "The Exercise of Primacy" given at Campion Hall in 1996, Archbishop John Quinn quoted these words which Archbishop Giovanni Benelli uttered while he was serving in the Roman Curia as Substitute Secretary of State:

> The real, effective jurisdiction of the pope over the whole Church is one thing. But centralization of power is another. The first is of divine law. The second is the result of human circumstances. The first has produced many good things. The second is an anomaly.

Protestants would of course have their doubts about what "effective jurisdiction" means. But they would say a loud "amen" to the peril of centralization. We have lived through a period of massive defections from national and international church headquarters. Consequently, today Protestants the world over are experimenting with all kinds of polity changes. Some will no doubt be disastrous. Others could work. And, as long as we keep reminding ourselves that the purpose of all church polity is ministry and service to the world, then these experiments might be useful for everyone.

V

I began these highly personal reflections on the papacy of the future with my early memory of the passing of Pius XI. I conclude with a much more recent papal encounter that also taught me a lot about Christian unity. In the summer of 1995, just weeks after the appearance of *Ut unum sint*, I was teaching in Rome at the same Waldensian Seminary on the Piazza Cavour where Cardinal Ratzinger would soon come to discuss the encyclical before an eager audience with the dean, Paulo Ricca. During that summer the pope held a smaller-than-usual audience after his return from Slovakia where, to the astonishment of his hosts, he had knelt in prayer at the grave of some Protestant martyrs. He wanted this particular audience to take place in St. Peter's Basilica itself, not in the new Hall of Audiences next door. It was a moving occasion. The pope obviously still had his recent visit in mind and he spoke eloquently about the need to put old dissensions and suspicions behind us and affirm what we hold in common. He then made a special point of greeting and shaking hands with the Protestant delegation of which I was part. When he took my hand he smiled as an aide told him of my connection with Harvard Divinity School where he had once given a lecture on phenomenology (which I regretfully admit I did not attend). He seemed a bit puzzled, however, and his brow knit when he learned that I was there with a delegation from the Waldensian Seminary in Rome. "Here," he asked, raising his eyebrows slightly, "in Rome?" Yes, I assured him, the seminary was indeed right here in Rome. It is hard for me to believe he did not know of its existence. Maybe he had simply forgotten, or was confused about why I should be there. But to me the symbolism seemed wonderfully appropriate. We were his neighbors.

Founded by Peter Waldo as the "Poor Men of Lyon," the Waldensian movement began two hundred years before the Reformation, at about the same time as the Franciscans, and embraced many of the same principles. They did not seek papal approval, however, as Francis had done, and immediately became one of the targets of the Inquisition. Most fled to the northern mountains of Italy or to remote regions of Sicily. Then, when Rome was incorporated into the new united Italy, some returned to Rome where they published the first Bible in Italian to appear in that city. They have been there—as well as in other parts of Italy—ever since. They like to point out to guests that their seminary, which adjoins a Waldensian church and a bookstore, stands within five hundred meters of the Vatican. I like to think that the presence at the audience of Waldensians from just across the Tiber reminded the pope that ecumenism is not just a matter of ecclesial diplomacy and encyclicals. It is also an issue for Main Street. To paraphrase my favorite Catholic politician, the man who represented my home district in Congress for many years, namely Tip O'Neill, all ecumenism is local. It is local or it isn't anything. The real test of *Ut unum sint* will be what happens between St. Patrick's parish in Malvern, where I first saw those mourning drapes, and the Baptist church down the street, and the A.M.E church across town. My hope is that the somber ribbons may be replaced by the garlands of a festive new chapter in ecumenism, one that inspires even the most remote churches to move together into the "new situation" with the kind of hope that can only come from the realization that Christ himself—not we ourselves—is the author of our unity, a unity that is intended to include not just the churches but the world God loves.

Contributors

Joan Chittister, Erie, Pennsylvania, a Benedictine Sister, is Executive Director of Benetvision, a resource center for contemporary spirituality. A national and international lecturer, she has a Ph.D. (Pennsylvania State University) and is a fellow of St. Edmund's College, Cambridge. She is the author of many books, including *There Is a Season* and *A Passion for Life* (both Orbis Books). Her latest book is *Heart of Flesh: A Feminist Spirituality for Women and Men* (Eerdmans).

Paul Collins, Canberra, Australia, is a priest, broadcaster, and historian. Born in Melbourne, Australia, he is a graduate of Harvard University and the Australian National University. His most recent book is *Papal Power* (HarperCollins, 1997).

Harvey Cox, Cambridge, Massachusetts, an ordained Baptist minister, is Thomas Professor of Divinity at Harvard University where he teaches courses on Theology, Ethics and Religion and Society. The author of *The Secular City*, his most recent book is *Fire from Heaven: The Rise of Pentecostal Spirituality and the Reshaping of Religion in the Twenty-first Century* (1995). He has lectured and taught widely both in Catholic and non-Catholic institutions, including the Gregorian University in Rome, and the Pontifical Catholic University of Peru.

Ana María Ezcurra, Buenos Aires, Argentina, is a psychologist with a Ph.D. in Latin America studies (National University of Mexico). She coordinates research on education and on society and religion at the Institute of Studies and Social Action in Buenos Aires. Her many books include several studies of Vatican politics.

Bernard Häring, C.Ss. R., Gars, Germany, is a Redemptorist priest and moral theologian. He taught for more than thirty years at the Academia Alfonsiana, Rome. He was a leading peritus (theological expert) at the Second Vatican Council and secretary of the commission that drafted *Gaudium et spes*, the Pastoral Constitution on the Church in the Modern World. A worldwide lecturer and retreat master, he has published more than eighty books, including *The Law of Christ* and *Free and Faithful in Christ*.

Gary MacEoin, San Antonio, Texas, has worked as a journalist in Ireland, Trinidad, and the United States, and has reported as a syndicated columnist from more than fifty countries worldwide. A lawyer, and a graduate of London University (Spanish, French) with a Ph.D. from the National University of Ireland (Spanish), he is a fellow of St. Edmund's College, Cambridge. His latest book is *The People's Church: Bishop Samuel Ruiz of Mexico and Why He Matters* (Crossroad).

Francis X. Murphy, C.Ss.R., Annapolis, Maryland, is a Redemptorist priest, born in New York, who served as a military chaplain and taught at the Academia Alfonsiana in Rome. As Xavier Rynne, he covered Vatican Council II for the *New Yorker* magazine and wrote a book on each session of the Council.

Pablo Richard, San José, Costa Rica, has licentiates in theology (from the Catholic University of Chile), and in sacred scripture (from the Pontifical Biblical Institute in Rome), and a doctorate in theology (from the University of Paris). He is a professor of theology at the National University of Costa Rica and a member of the Department of Ecumenical Investigations (DEI), Costa Rica. His books include *Death of Christendoms, Birth of the Church*.

John Wilkins, London, has been editor of the international Catholic weekly, *The Tablet*, since 1982. Previously he worked for ten years in the BBC's External Services as a scriptwriter and broadcaster. Born in Cheltenham, England, in 1936, he obtained his BA degree from Cambridge University in 1961. Books he has edited include *Understanding Veritatis Splendor* (London: SPCK).

Alain Woodrow, Paris, is a graduate of Oxford University (French, Russian) and of Saint Sulpice (theology). He was an editor of *Pax Romana Journal* (Fribourg, Switzerland) and *Informations Catholiques Internationales* (Paris), and religion editor of *Le Monde* (Paris), and has authored seven books; the most recent, in English, is *The Jesuits: A Story of Power* (London: Geoffrey Chapman).

Giancarlo Zizola, Rome, dean of Vaticanologists, has covered the Vatican for publications in many countries since before the Vatican Council. Many of his books have been translated into the major European languages; two of them, biographies of John XXIII and Paul VI, into English.